Colorado's Forks in th

An Adventurer's Guide to Unique

Maybe it started when I was very young growing up in a small town in Western Colorado in the 50's and watching my mom making a perfect baked Alaska dessert. Or possibly it was the many weekend ski trips with their 3 hour Sunday night drives home stopping at small inns and restaurants along the way for cozy family dinners after wonderful times in the Rocky Mountain snow. Whatever it was, I have always been fascinated by food and restaurants, especially hidden, remote and hard to find restaurants. After 35 years in the restaurant business I still love finding these hidden restaurant gems and meeting the amazingly independent characters that are the proprietors of these places, and of course trying all the diverse menus.

The arrival of the Interstate System in America signaled the demise of a lot of unique, cozy and romantic restaurants of the old days. I sometimes wonder what the country would be like if chain restaurants and the Interstate System had never come upon the scene. What an amazing variety of restaurants we would be experiencing. But, before I make you too sad, there is good news. I have spent the last year cruising the highways and byways of Colorado for the remaining hidden, hard to find and out of the way restaurants and inns. I have found them; a lot of these places still remain.

This book is a way to showcase the strong and independent individuals who chose to ply their trade in remote, hard to find places in Colorado. What would we do without these incredible people who make our lives so enjoyable as we tour this great state of Colorado? Imagine if you, the adventurer in you, were traveling through our stunning beautiful parks; forests and monuments and there were no unique shops, inns and restaurants along the way. This is a part of Colorado that I hope to show you. There are places and experiences that you'll enjoy on this amazing tour. Turn the page and journey into my book — enjoy!

Table of *Contents*

ISBN: 978-0-9794695-0-3

Photography by Reginald Barbour

Graphic Design by Bobbie Van Meter

Dedication

I am dedicating this to my friends and family for being so supportive while I changed my career and pursued my dream of writing books about out of the way, fun and interesting places where people can enjoy something a little different in their lives.

My mom, Evelyn, always said to follow your dreams before its too late and the dream dies within you. I owe my wife Mary so much for supporting this project and standing behind me all the way. Thanks, also, to the restaurant owners and staff for their enthusiasm for the idea and their pride in being selected, which kept me motivated and inspired to finish it. Thanks also to the wonderful and talented Bobbie Van Meter, without whose assistance, there would be no book.

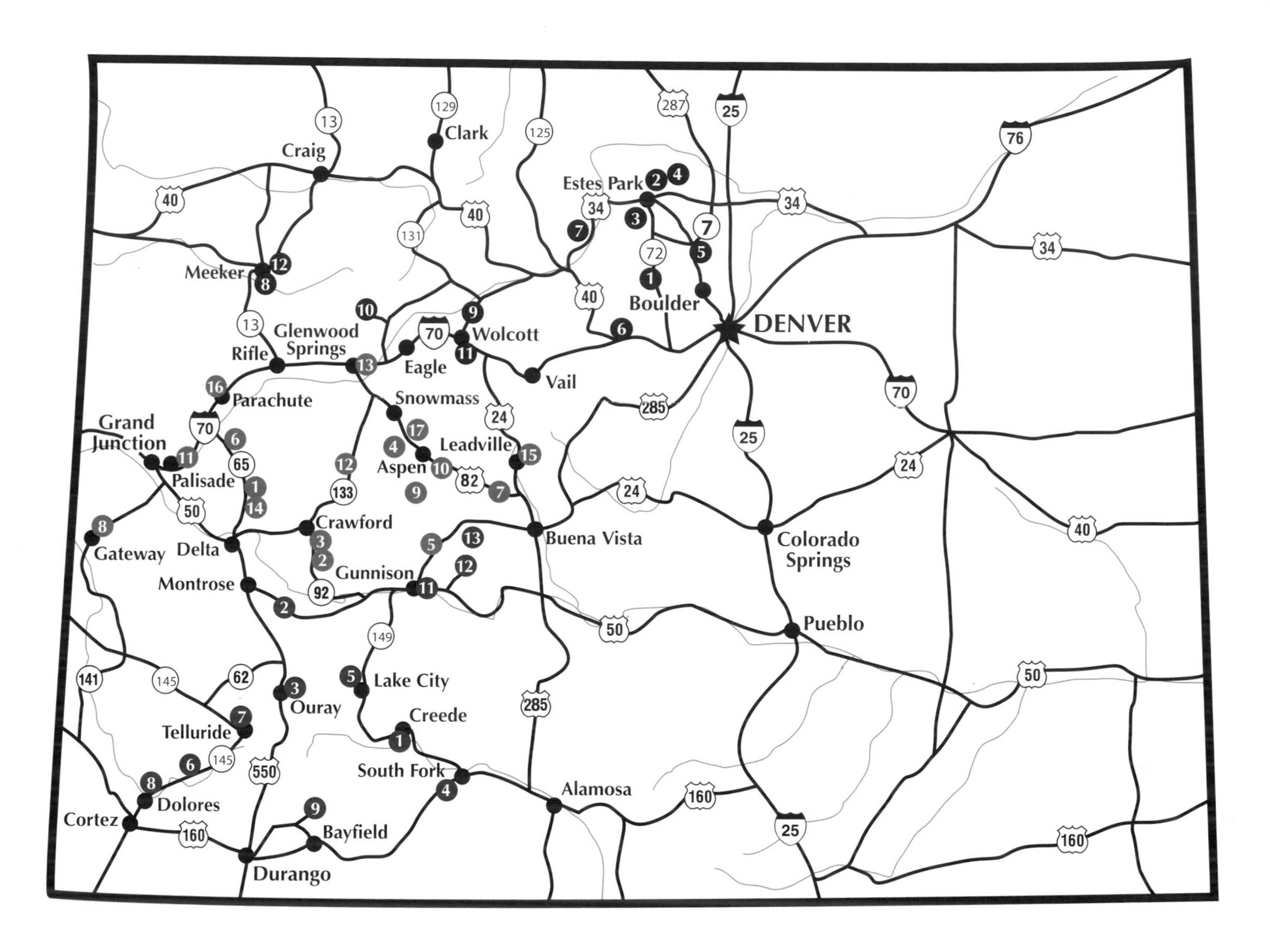
Craig
Clark
Estes Park
Meeker
Boulder
DENVER
Glenwood
Springs
Rifle
Wolcott
Eagle
Vail
Parachute
Snowmass
Grand
Junction
Leadville
Aspen
Palisade
Crawford
Buena Vista
Colorado
Springs
Gateway
Delta
Gunnison
Montrose
Pueblo
Lake City
Ouray
Creede
Telluride
South Fork
Alamosa
Dolores
Cortez
Bayfield
Durango

Colorado Regional Map

Northern Colorado

1. Alice's Restaurant at Gold Lake Mountain Resort & Spa *(Ward)*
2. The Baldpate Inn *(Estes Park)*
3. The Fawn Brook Inn *(Allenspark)*
4. Inn Of Glen Haven *(Glen Haven)*
5. La Chaumiere *(Lyons)*
6. The Peck House *(Empire)*
7. The Rapids Lodge and Restaurant *(Grand Lake)*
8. Sleepy Cat Guest Ranch *(Meeker)*
9. State Bridge Lodge & Resort *(Bond)*
10. Sweetwater Lake Resort *(Sweetwater)*
11. The Yacht Club *(Walcott)*
12. Trappers Lake Lodge & Resort *(Meeker)*

Southern Colorado

1. Antlers Rio Grande Lodge & Riverside Restaurant *(Creede)*
2. The Inn At Arrowhead *(Cimmaron)*
3. Bachelor Syracuse Mine *(Ouray)*
4. Chalet Swiss *(South Fork)*
5. The Crystal Lodge & Restaurant *(Lake City)*
6. Dunton Hot Springs *(Dunton)*
7. Elk Mountain Resort *(Telluride)*
8. Old Germany Restaurant *(Dolores)*
9. Virginia's Steakhouse *(Vallecito)*
10. Wits End Guest Ranch & Resort *(Durango)*
11. Pappy's On The Lake Restaurant *(Gunnison)*
12. Road Kill Cafe *(Pitkin)*
13. Frenchy's on the Pond *(Tincup)*

Central Colorado

1. Alexander Lake Lodge *(Cedaredge)*
2. The Boardwalk Restaurant *(Crawford)*
3. Branding Iron Steak House *(Crawford)*
4. Butch's Lobster Bar *(Snowmass Village)*
5. Harmels Resort *(Almont)*
6. Mesa Lakes Resort *(Mesa)*
7. The Nordic Inn *(Twin Lakes)*
8. The Paradox Grille *(Gateway)*
9. The Pine Creek Cookhouse *(Ashcroft)*
10. Poppies Bistro Cafe *(Aspen)*
11. Red Rose Cafe *(Palisade)*
12. The Redstone Inn *(Redstone)*
13. The Rivers Restaurant *(Glenwood Springs)*
14. The Spruce Lodge *(Cedaredge)*
15. The Grill Bar & Cafe *(Leadville)*
16. White Buffalo West *(Battlement Mesa)*
17. Woody Creek Tavern *(Woody Creek)*

10
9

Northern Colorado

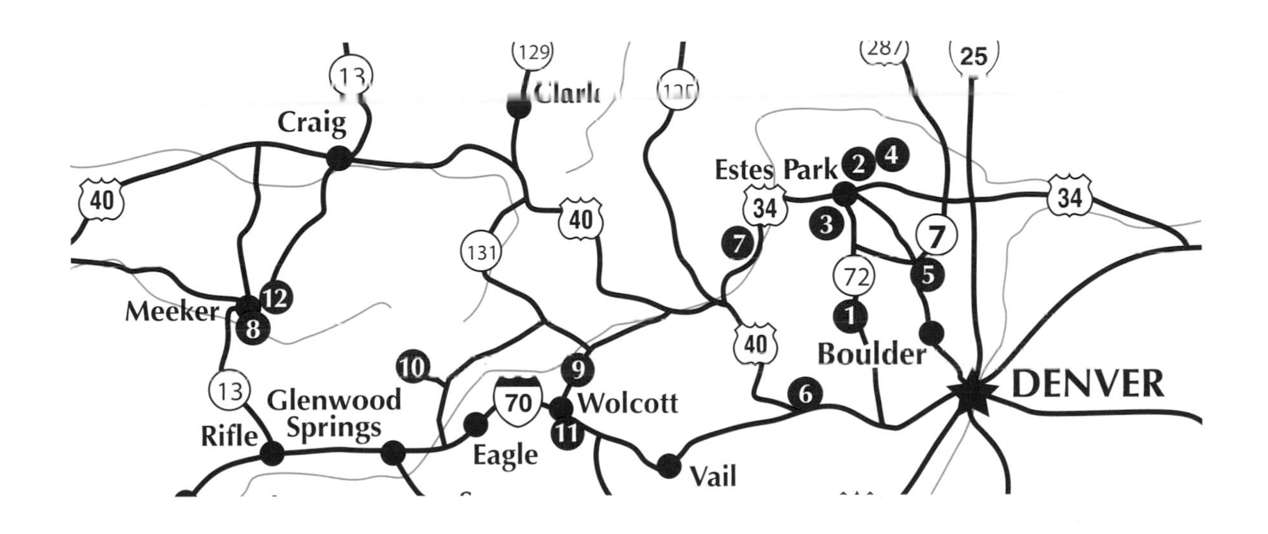

Alice's Restaurant At Gold Mountain Resort

Ward, Colorado

Gold Lake is a magical mountain getaway, situated on 100 acres just 25 miles northwest of Boulder, Colorado. Gold Lake Mountain Resort & Spa offers a truly unique experience with lakeside hot pools, artistically restored cabins, great spa therapies and the romantic award winning Alice's Restaurant.

Alice's Restaurant serves savory "Mountain Spa Cuisine" in their historic log lodge featuring an oversized stone fireplace and stunning views of the Continental Divide. Their "Swiss Continental Breakfast" features; house-made yogurt, granola, breads and pastries, along with fresh juices, hot items, and organic, fresh-ground Sumatra coffees. Lunches feature casual entrees, starting with a cup of fresh hot soup or a refreshing salad.

Alice's menu changes all the time and it includes appetizers like Baby Spinach Salad, Shrimp and Scallop Cakes with roasted red pepper and toasted almond aioli, or Crisp Pastry Puff with asparagus, parmesan, fresh herbs and sherry vinaigrette. Entrée samples are Almond Crusted Flounder, Farmers Cheese Orechietti, Marinated Grilled Venison, Pan Seared Halibut, Crispy Duck Breast with Ratatouille or Spicy Thai Stir-Fry. For dessert, try Warm Flourless Chocolate Cake with Caramelized Bananas, Gingerbread Cake, Chocolate Mousse or Strawberry and Rhubarb Tarts. In the bar try their Sauza Margaritas, Cruzan Rum Mojitos or Passion Fruit infused Cognac Cocktails.

CONTACT US

[303] 459-3544
3371 Gold Lake Road
Ward, Co. 80481
E-Mail: goldlake@goldlake.com
Web Site: www.goldlake.com

WHAT'S COOKING

Mountain Spa Cuisine

HOW TO GET HERE

From Ward take Co. 72 north 0.3 miles. Turn right on Gold lake Road go 2.7 miles.

AREA ACTIVITIES

Horseback Riding
Hiking
Mountain Biking
Fly-Fishing
Back Country Skiing
Canoeing
Kayaking
Ice Skating
Swimming

AREA INFORMATION

City Guide for Ward Colorado
enwikipedia.org/wiki/ward

Boulder Colorado Visitor Bureau
www.bouldercoloradousa.com

The Baldpate Inn

Estes Park, Colorado

Located in the beautiful mountains just south of Estes Park. The Inn's private 15 acres are surrounded by Rocky Mountain Park and National Forest lands. Built in 1917 The Baldpate Inn is perched on the side of Twin Sisters Mountain at an altitude of 9,000 feet.

The Baldpate Inn was named after the mystery novel, Seven Keys to Baldpate by Earl Derr Biggers. In the novel, each of the guests think they have the only key. In keeping with the story line of the novel, the Inn gave each visitor their own key. The loyal guests who returned yearly were so disappointed that the tradition was broken due to the increase in the cost of metal during World War 1, that they began their own tradition of bringing a key back to the inn. A display was made and it has grown to over 20,000. Included are keys from the Pentagon, Westminster Abby, Mozart's wine cellar and even Frankenstein's castle to name a few.

For more than 20 years the Baldpate's dining room was rated as a 5-star Duncan Hines restaurant. Today they continue the tradition of providing an unparalleled dining experience in their specialty restaurant. The restaurant is open to the public from 11:30am-8:00pm. daily. The Baldpate operates from Memorial Day weekend to mid October.

The cozy main dining room, has the feel of log and lace, a mountain hunting lodge with its classic stone fireplace, antique hickory chairs, and views of the surrounding forest. They have become quite famous for their fresh salad bar as well as their homemade soups. breads, and pies.

The Baldpate serves a three-course breakfast which features; coffee and fruit juice, homemade muffins, seasonal berries, homemade Quiche, and hot home-baked cinnamon rolls fresh from the oven. They also cater special meetings, luncheons, weddings, receptions, and dinner parties for groups up to 100 people.

CONTACT US:

[970] 586-6151
P.O. Box 700
4900 South Hwy. 7
Estes Park, Co. 80517
E-Mail: baldpateinn@aol.com
Web Site:www.baldpateinn.com

WHAT'S COOKING

American Regional Cuisine

HOW TO GET HERE

Located seven miles south of Estes Park on Hwy. 7

AREA ACTIVITIES

Boating on Lake Estes
Summer music festivals
Golfing
Hiking
Fishing
Hunting
Biking

AREA INFORMATION

Estes Park Chamber of Commerce
www.estesparkresort.com

Estes Park Welcome Center
www.estespark.com

Estes Park Restaurant & Lodge
www,estespark.us

The Fawn Brook Inn

Allenspark, Colorado

The Fawn Brook Inn is located in Allenspark, 17 miles northeast of the town of Boulder. This romantic restaurant is located on the Peak-to-Peak Scenic highway 7, which stretches 55 miles along the Colorado mountaintops from Central City to Estes Park.

At the Fawn Brook Inn, dinners start with appetizers like; Escargot, Seafood Maison [tender king crab meat, baby langostinos, jumbo sea scallops and lobster, lighly napped with sauce Remolade]. Also, Game Pate with lingonberries, Beefsteak Tartare prepared tableside or Caesar Salad also prepared tableside.

Entrees at the Fawn Brook include; Roast Duck, Cote de Veau Normandy, Black Forest Beef Rouladen, Vegetarian Plates, Lamb Medallions, Steak au Poivre, Shrimp Provencal, Dover Sole a la Meniere and Curried Lobster and Seafood En Croute. The Fawn Brook also serves dinners for two, tableside. These dinners include Chateaubriand, Filet of Beef Wellington and Rack of Lamb.

CONTACT US

[303] 747-2556
387 Highway 7 Business Loop
Allenspark, Colorado 80510

WHAT'S COOKING

French Continental

HOW TO GET HERE

Located 17 miles northeast of Boulder on the scenic peak to peak Hwy. 7.

AREA ACTIVITIES

Horseback Riding
Cross Country Skiing
Hiking
ATV'S
Snowshoeing
Romantic Getaways

AREA INFORMATION

Allenspark Colorado
www.allenspark.com

Allenspark Lodging, Camping
coloradodirectory.com

Allenspark Travel and Visitor Information
www.colorado.com/city29

The Inn Of Glen Haven

Glen Haven, Colorado

The Inn of Glen Haven has been faithfully restored to reflect its original charm, this old world retreat maintains the romantic atmosphere of an intimate English country inn. Surrounded by the beautiful Rocky Mountains miles seven north of the town of Estes Park on Devil's Gulch, the Inn is minutes away from Rocky Mountain National Park.

The individually decorated rooms preserve the original character of the Inn. Suites range from Victorian motif to the Colonial era. The Inn of Glen Haven serves dinner every night from 5:30-9:00 except Tuesday. All dinners are served in the intimate antique filled dining room. You can also relax in the parlor with its huge stone fireplace, or search for the hidden wine cellar while partaking of the pub's libations.

Appetizers at Glen Haven start with; Seared Sea Scallops " Rockefeller", Crab Stuffed Mushrooms, Melted Brie with Fresh Fruit and Baguettes, Escargot De Café Paris, or Shrimp Cocktail. Entrees include Steak Escoffier, Pecan Chicken, Black and Blue Loin of Elk, Bacon Wrapped Pork, Duck a L'Orange, Filet of Halibut [topped with two large shrimp, artichoke hearts and a creamy tarragon sauce] and Stuffed Trout.

During the twelve days of Christmas, the Inn serves a traditional Old English menu that includes; Whole Roast Suckling Pig, Special Roast of Fowl, Beef, and Lamb, along with Flaming Plum Pudding.

CONTACT US
[970] 586-3897
7168 County Road 43
P.O. Box 219
Glen Haven, Colorado 80532
www.info@glenhaven.com

WHAT'S COOKING
Gourmet Continental

HOW TO GET HERE
Located 7 miles north of Estes Park on County Road 41

AREA ACTIVITIES
Fishing
Hiking
Scenic Drives
Golfing
Watching Wildlife
Rock Climbing
Cross Country Skiing
Horseback Riding
Historical Tours
Backpacking

AREA INFORMATION
Estes Park Welcome Center
www.estes-park.com

Estes Park Virtual Visitor Guide
www.estesnet.com

Estes Park Chamber Resort Assn.
www.estesparkresorts.com

La Chaumiere
Lyons, Colorado

Are you looking for a place to have a quiet romantic dinner? Or maybe a place to celebrate an anniversary or ask that special someone to spend the rest of their life with you? Or just a restaurant that offers tranquil mountain vistas in an elegant setting? La Chaumiere, located west on highway 36 in Pinewood Springs, outside Lyons, is just that place.

Nestled in the foothills along Colorado's front range, La Chaumiere has been offering beautifully presented, yet unpretentious, French cuisine in a spectacular mountain setting for over thirty years. La Chaumiere is open Tuesday through Saturday 5:30p.m-10:00p.m. and 4:00p.m.-9:00p.m. on Sunday.

Start your meal at La Chaumiere with appetizers such as; Duck Liver Pate or Wild Boar Ravioli [ravioli stuffed with wild boar, completed with a Chasseur sauce]. They also have Artichoke Dip, Escargot's A La Bourguigonne, Baked Brie in Puff Pastry with Raspberry sauce or their award winning Maryland Crab Soup.

Entrees include; Sauteed Sweetbreads with a fine Herb Demi-Glaze, Lavender Crusted Poussin "tender young chicken crusted with lavender, roasted over an open fire and served with an Apricot Glaze", Rocky Mountain Trout, Filet Mignon and Stuffed Quail. Specials of the day include Pan Seared Scallops, Fresh Hudson Valley Foie Gras, Stuffed Calamari, Striped Bass, Frog Legs and Veal Rib Chops. Desserts are decadent here and include Bananas Foster, Death by Chocolate, Crème Brulee and White and Dark Chocolate Mousse.

CONTACT US

[303] 823-6521
12311 N. Saint Vrain Dr.
Lyons, Colorado 80540
E-Mail: vince1212@msn.com
www.lachaumiere-restaurant.com

WHAT'S COOKING

French Cuisine

HOW TO GET HERE

Located 8 miles west of Lyons, on Hwy. 36 in Pinedale

AREA ACTIVITIES

Horseback Riding
Fishing
Hunting
Golfing
Hiking
Rafting
Biking

AREA INFORMATION

Lyons Colorado Chamber of Commerce
www.lyons-colorado.com

Town of Lyons Colorado
www.townoflyons.com

Lyons Colorado
www.downtownlyons.com

The Peck House

Empire, Colorado

Located high in the Colorado Mountains in the small town of Empire, the Peck House is the oldest continuously running hotel and restaurant in the state. Rated 5 star, the owner Chef has won the Colorado Governor's Award for Colorado Cuisine.

Built in 1862, the Peck House has 11 Victorian rooms with private baths, in house Jacuzzi, bar and lounge, gourmet restaurant and complimentary breakfast.

The Peck House dinner highlights include; Steak Au Poivre, Veal a la Peck, Steak Bearnaise, Raspberry Duck, Brace of Quail, New Zealand Red Deer in a Cabernet and Brandy sauce and Beef and Oyster Pie. On the Fish and Seafood side, special items are Trout Clara Lu [stuffed with rice, artichoke and baby shrimp, topped with hollandaise sauce]. Shrimp Sarah, Shrimp Napoleon Chardonnay and Macadamia Salmon.

Every Friday and Saturday night the Peck House has special dinners entrees. These entrees include; Beef Wellington, Steak Italiano, Herb Encrusted Lamb, Venison Steak with a Cherry Cabernet Sauce and Chicken Alfredo. On Sunday nights they feature Seafood Specials. These specials include Scallops Vera Cruz, Salmon Oscar, Crayfish Jambalaya, Stuffed Shrimp with Orange Hollandaise, Trout and Walleye Amaretto and Live Maine Lobsters.

CONTACT US
[303] 569-9870
83 Sunny Ave.
P.O. Box 428
Empire, Colorado 80438
www.thepeckhouse.com

WHAT'S COOKING
Gourmet Continental

HOW TO GET HERE
From Denver, take I-70 west to exit 232. Go 2 miles on Highway 40 to the town of Empire. Then go 2/3 of the way through town.

AREA ACTIVITIES
Narrow Gauge Railroad
Skiing
Casinos
Fishing
Gold Panning
Hiking
Backpacking
Cross Country Skiing

AREA INFORMATION
Empire, Colorado Home
www.empire-colorado.com

Historic Georgetown
www.historicgeorgetown.org

Georgetown, Colorado Visitor Info
www.townofGeorgetown,co.us

The Rapids Lodge and Restaurant

Grand Lake, Colorado

The historic Rapids Lodge and Restaurant is located on the banks of the beautiful Tonahutu River. It was built in 1915, and is tucked away in the quaint village of Grand Lake, on the west side of Rocky Mountain National Park. [The City of Grand Lake is on the eastern end of Grand Lake, the largest natural lake in Colorado.] The city is truely one of Colorado's great unspoiled hideaways.

The Rapids Lodge rents cabins, condos, lodge rooms and suites. In the 1950's the second floor of the historic building was a casino and the third floor was a brothel. During the 60's Jim Croce, Kris Kristofferson and Janis Joplin all played at the Rapids when it was a thriving Honky Tonk Bar. There is a friendly old lady ghost that wanders the corridors, moves and hides items and opens and closes doors. She used to drink a bit they say and one day her husband just disappeared and was never found.

The Rapids serves dinner daily in the summer and Wednesday thru Sunday in the winter. The full service lounge and the dinning room open at 5:00p.m. The restaurant is closed April and November.

All entrees at the Rapids include their famous Shrimp Appetizer tray, Rapids Salad, or Soup of the Day' Chef's Accompaniments, Fresh Bread and Sorbet. The menu specialties include; Rapids Tournados, Grilled New York, Pan Seared Elk Medallions, Loin of Lamb And Pine Nut Crusted Atlantic Salmon. Additional Specialties are Shitake Crusted Halibut, Fresh Seafood Skewers, Pork Chops and stuffed Portabello Mushrooms. They also offer fresh Desserts of the evening and Prime Rib on Thursdays and Friday. The Rapids also provide a full bar and an extensive wine list.

CONTACT US

[970] 627-3707
209 Rapids Lane
Grand Lake, Colorado 80447
www.rapidslodge.com

WHAT'S COOKING

American Regional Cuisine

HOW TO GET HERE

Take Hwy. 34 from Granby to Grand Lake. Follow Grand Ave. through town to Hancock St. Turn left and go one and a half blocks to the Rapids Lodge.

AREA ACTIVITIES

Golf
Hiking
Horses
Fishing
Rafting
Boating
Mini-Golf
Mountain Biking
Alpine Slide

AREA INFORMATION

Grand Lake Chamber of Commerce
www.grandlakechamber.com

Grand Lake Colorado Virtual Tour
www.grandlake.com/co

Grand Lake/Rocky Mountain National Park
www.grand-county.com/grandlakeaspx

Sleepy Cat Guest Ranch

Meeker, Colorado

Sleepy Cat Ranch is located 17 miles east of Meeker, Colorado in the scenic White River Valley. They are located on the Flat Tops Scenic Byway, just a few miles from the Flat Tops Wilderness Area and the White River National Forest. Across the road is the Oak Ridge State Wildlife Area.

Sleepy Cat offers a full service bar and lounge, and also has cabins, motel rooms and a liquor store. The restaurant is located at the base of Sleepy Cat Mountain and offers spectacular views as you sit and dine in their cozy and inviting lodge.

The appetizer list features; Crabs Cakes with Remoulade Sauce, Sesame Beef Bowls, Salmon Rillette, and Cajun Barbequed Shrimp. Favorite dinner entrees include; Rib Eye Steaks, Filet Mignon, Slow Roasted Prime Rib, London Broil, Elk Medallions or Kansas City Strip Steak. Other specialties are Grilled Game Hens, King Crab Legs, Lobster, Rocky Mountain Baked Trout, Whiskey Creek Salmon and Barbecued Baby Back Ribs.

CONTACT US

[970] 878-4413
16064 County Road 8
Meeker, Colorado 11641
E-Mail:
info@sleepycatguestranch.com
www.sleepycatguestranch.com

WHAT'S COOKING

Continental

Located 18 miles east of Meeker
on County Road 8

AREA ACTIVITIES

Fishing
Hunting
Snowmobiling
Cross Country Skiing
Horse Back Riding
Backpacking
4 Wheeling
Biking

AREA INFORMATION

Meeker Chamber of Commerce
www.meekerchamber.com

Town of Meeker
www.townofmeeker.org

Meeker Colorado and the White
River
www.meelercolorado.com

State Bridge Lodge
Bond, Colorado

The historic State Bridge Lodge and River Resort has over 24 acres of fun in the middle of an outdoor enthusiasts dream, on the headwaters of the beautiful Colorado River. On the weekends they host world class musical acts on their deck overlooking the river.

State Bridge is open daily from 8:30 a.m. to 10:00 p.m. close and serves breakfast, lunch and dinner. Breakfast includes; Eggs, Pancakes, Breakfast Burritos, French Toast, Omelets, and an item called Gallo Pinto [a Costa Rican staple, eggs, black beans, blended cheeses, tomatoes, cabbage] served with a side of veggie green chili and rice, beans & topped with avocado.

Lunch and dinner start with a wide range of appetizers, examples are; Buffalo Fingers, Fried Calamari, Quesadillas, Chicken Wings, Nachos, Buckets of Peel & Eat Shrimp, Garden Veggies, a Buddah Wrap, Ute Smoked Trout and Veggie Pot Stickers. Sandwiches include Burgers, Blackened Mahi Mahi, BBQ Chicken, Fried Green Tomato BLT's and Grilled Cheese.

CONTACT US

[970] 653-4444
127 Trough Road
Bond, Colorado 80423
Web Site: www.statebridge.com

WHAT'S COOKING

High Country Southwest

HOW TO GET HERE

Take I-70 West to Exit 157 [Wolcott], then take Co. 131 north toward Steamboat Springs for 14 miles. Cross the Colorado State Bridge, the lodge is on the right.

AREA ACTIVITIES

Rafting
Fishing
Hiking
Kayaking
Floating
Biking
Hunting
Exploring Dinosaur Tracks

AREA INFORMATION

Wolcott, Co. City Guide
local.yahoo.com/co/walcott

Vail Valley Tourism
www.vailalways.com

Steamboat Springs Chamber
www.sreamboatchamber.com

Diamond Jack's Western Restaurant

Sweetwater, Colorado

Sweetwater Lake Resort is on the edge of the Flat Tops Wilderness area, 7,700 feet up in the grandeur of the White River National Forest. Another world exists here at Sweetwater and so does Diamond Jack's Western Restaurant.

At Diamond Jack's an unforgettable panorama of nature unfolds before you. Enjoy a leisurely evening dinner on the deck of the restaurant overlooking Sweetwater Lake as the rainbow and german trout jump as if they were reaching for the sky.

Breakfast at Diamond Jack's features the basics; Bacon, Sausage, Pancakes and Omelets. Lunch features Bison Burgers from a nearby ranch and at dinner you can get steaks, chicken and arguably the best Chicken Fried Steak in Colorado. For dessert the restaurant has the finest home made pies you'll ever try, don't forget the ice cream.

Sweetwater Lake Resort offers cabins, Motel/Hotel rooms with cooking facilities, tent camping and RV camping. Some cabins are on the lake and include fireplaces and decks. The resort also features rainbow and german brown trout, as well as kokanee salmon fishing in both the lake and nearby streams. Available on site are rowboat and canoe rentals, a barbecue picnic area, volleyball court and horseshoe area. There's even a wilderness cooking and packing school here! Nearby activities include a museum, golf course, whitewater rafting tours, and snowmobile trails. Tour the historic Ute Indian cave found on the resort's property and view the pictographs. Diamond Jack's serves breakfast, lunch and dinner daily.

CONTACT US

[970]-524-7344
Fax: [970] 524-7346
3406 Sweetwater Road
Sweetwater, Colorado 81637
E-Mail: info@brinkoutfitters.com
www.brinkoutfitters.com

WHAT'S COOKING

Western Steakhouse

HOW TO GET HERE

From I-70 take the Dotsero Exit 133 north for 7 miles to Anderson's Camp. Turn west and follow Sweetwater Creek 10 miles.

AREA ACTIVITIES

Horseback Riding
Picnics
Fishing
Photography Trips
Hunting
Hiking Climbing
Ice Fishing
Cross Country Skiing
Cowboy Golf

AREA INFORMATION

Vail Valley Chamber and Tourism
www.visitvailvalley.com

Glenwood Springs Chamber
Resort Association
www.glenwoodchamber.com

The Yacht Club Grill

Wolcott, Colorado

Located just 10 miles west of Beaver Creek, along the Colorado River, sits the Yacht Club Grill in the midst of the most picturesque landscapes in the Vail Valley. It sits in the center of one of the most famous Gold Medal trout fishing areas in the state.

The Yacht Club serves breakfast from 7a.m.-11a.m. and lunch/dinner 11a.m.-9p.m. In the summer months with live music on Friday nights the club is the place to be in the Vail Valley.

Breakfast highlights include; Steak & Eggs, Omelets, Homemade Biscuits & Gravy, Burritos and Huevos Rancheros.

The Club serves the same menu for lunch and dinner. For starters try Calamari, Peanut Chicken Skewers, Miranda's Coconut Shrimp, or a Caesar Salad with your choice of Ahi Tuna, Chicken or Salmon. They also have Vegetarian entrees and a childrens menu.

Entrée favorites are; Fish Tacos, Oyster Po'Boy, Catfish Po'Boy, and wild caught Grilled Salmon. The Yacht Club also serves up 8oz. Angus Burgers and a variety of sandwiches such as Cuban Roast Pork, Gyros, Portobello, Brie Apple and Walnut, and Eggplant, Zucchini and Tomato. Leave room for dessert. The Key lime pie and Oliver Twist finish out a nice meal at this wonderful Grill.

CONTACT US

[970] 926-3444
27190 U.S. Hwy. 6
Wolcott, Colorado 81657

WHAT'S COOKING

American

HOW TO GET HERE

On I-70 take Exit 157 toward Co. 131 Wolcott/Steamboat Springs. Go 0.2 miles, turn left on Hwy. 6, Yacht Club is on the left.

AREA ACTIVITIES

Hiking
Biking
Skiing
Fishing
Kayaking
Rafting
Golfing
Horse Back Riding

AREA INFORMATION

Vail Resort
ci.vail.co.us

Vail Valley Tourism
www.vailalways.com

Beaver Creek Resort
Beavercreek.snow.com

Trappers Lake Lodge & Resort

Meeker, Colorado

50 miles east of Meeker in the middle of the White River National Forest and bordering the Flat Tops Wilderness Area lies Trappers Lake Lodge. In operation since 1922, Trappers Lake is the 2nd largest natural lake in Colorado, spawning its own Cutthroat Trout. It's a fly fishermen's paradise. The area features over 30 alpine lakes with 1,400 surface acres. At 9,500 feet breakfast, lunch and dinner would have to be described as high altitude dining.

Breakfast features; Omelet's, Flapjacks, Waffles, Bacon, Sausage, Fresh Fruit or Biscuits and Gravy. For lunch at Trappers, enjoy a great mountain meal in the restaurant or out on the deck, and watch as wildlife strolls by. Try the homemade soup of the day or a fresh garden salad. You can also choose Chicken Fried Steak, Hamburgers, Veggie Burgers and Chicken Breast Sandwiches. Relax and enjoy your meal as you choose your options for the day in this pristine wilderness.

In the evening at Trappers Lake, enjoy outstanding and unpretentious service, mouthwatering meals, the rustic cozy atmosphere, and the knowledge that you are surrounded by over 300,000 acres of wilderness. Each night the staff offers an evening special. It may include Pot Roast, Salmon, Baked Chicken, Roast Pork, BBQ Ribs, Lasagna, Fettuccini or Hand Cut Steaks. Trappers also has a full bar with wine and champagne, so you can sit around and boast about that big fish that got away.

CONTACT US

[970] 878-3336
7700 Trappers Lake Road
Meeker, Colorado 81641
E Mail: info@trapperslake.com
Web Site: www.trapperslake.com

WHAT'S COOKING

American

HOW TO GET HERE

39 miles East of Meeker on County Road 8, "Flat Top Scenic Byway". Then 11 miles on Trappers Lake Road 205.

AREA ACTIVITIES

Fishing
Boating
Canoeing
Kayaking
Hiking
Biking
Hunting

AREA INFORMATION

Meeker Chamber of Commerce
www.meekerchamber.com

Meeker and the White River Valley
wwwmeekercolorado.com

Guide to Western Colorado's Outdoor Activities
www.colorado-west.com

Central Colorado

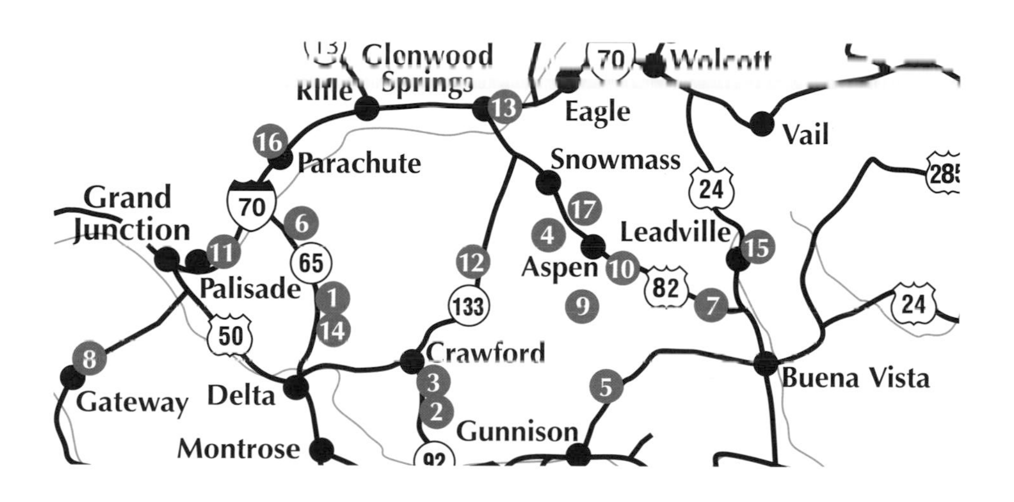

Alexander Lake Lodge
Mesa, Colorado

On the very top of the highest flat top mountain in the world and surrounded by over 300 alpine lakes sits Alexander Lake Lodge. Its ambiance and views are a must to experience. The lodge is nearly 100 years old. Its history is rich, colorful, and filled with the excitement of the first ever lodge built high atop this colorful Colorado mountain. The lodge rests on 10 private acres and is surrounded by 360,000 acres of U.S. Forest lands.

Alexander's serves Breakfast, Lunch and Dinner every day of the week. The menu selections are small but the quality of the food and ambiance of the 100 year old lodge, plus the spectacular scenery, are worth the drive. Breakfast selections include; Eggs, Hash Browns, Bacon and Sausage, French Toast, Biscuits and Gravy and Ham and Cheese Omelets.

Lunches at Alexander Lake Lodge feature Homemade Red and Green Chili, Beef and Bean Burritos, Mini Pizzas, Hot Dogs and a selection of Burgers. They also have a kids menu. Dinners start with Mozzarella Sticks, Texas Toothpicks, Fried Zucchini, Battered Mushrooms or a combination of any. Dinner entrees include Chicken Fried Steak with Country Gravy, New York Strip Steak, Coulotte Steak, Marinated Chicken Breast, Smothered Burritos and Halibut or Salmon.

CONTACT US

[970] 856-6240
[800] 850-7221
2121 AA50 Road
Cedaredge, Colorado 81413
E-Mail: rhazen@alexander.com
Web Site: alexanderlakelodge.com

WHAT'S COOKING

American

HOW TO GET HERE

2 miles east of the Grand Mesa Visitor Center off Hwy. 65

AREA ACTIVITIES

Scenic Byways
Fishing
Biking Trails
Hiking
Skiing
Cross Country Skiing
Snowmobiling
Photography

AREA INFORMATION

Grand Mesa, Colorado Cabins, Lodging and Camping
www.coloradodirectly.com

Grand Mesa National Scenic Byway
www.grandmesabyway.org

Cedaredge Area Chamber of Commerce
www.cedaredge.com

The Boardwalk Restaurant

Crawford, Colorado

Nestled up against the West Elk Mountain range and a short distance from the world famous Black Canyon of the Gunnison National Park, lies the Boardwalk Restaurant. It's in the authentic old western town of Crawford. The restaurant serves Breakfast, Lunch, Dinner and has a full separate bar.

Breakfast features; Steak & Eggs, Breakfast Cut Pork Chops, Omelets, Pancakes, Waffles and big homemade, old fashioned Cinnamon Rolls. Lunch is all about Hamburgers, with tons of different choices. Other standouts on the lunch menu include Veggie Verde sandwich, Philly Cheese Steak, Burritos and Gigantic Navajo Tacos.

Dinners at the Boardwalk are all about steaks, starting with 3 sizes of Sirloin; 4oz., 6oz. and 8oz. Then there's an 8oz. Filet Mignon, a 10oz. Rib Eye, a 12oz. NY Strip a 16oz. T-Bone and a 12oz. Prime Rib. They also serve; Broiled Chicken, Teriyaki Chicken, Pork Chops, Liver and Onions and Filet of Salmon. For Dessert try the homemade fruit pies, cream pies and cream cheese pies.

CONTACT US

[970] 921-4905
[970] 921-3777
P.O. Box 25
64 Hwy. 92
Crawford, Colorado 81415

WHAT'S COOKING

American

HOW TO GET HERE

Located on the south side of Crawford, on Hwy. 92

AREA ACTIVITIES

Fishing
Camping
Water Skiing
Swimming
Hunting
Hiking
Biking
Trail Riding

AREA INFORMATION

Crawford Chamber of Commerce
www.craefordcountry.org

Crawford Colorado Tourist Attractions
www.planetware.com

Black Canyon of the Gunnison National Park
www.nps.gov/blca

The Branding Iron Steakhouse

Crawford, Colorado

This quaint and rustic steakhouse is located in the authentic old western town of Crawford. Crawford is only 16 miles north of the north rim of the Black Canyon National Park. The park offers breathtaking views of one of the United States deepest canyons and the pristine Gunnison River.

Lunch at the Branding Iron is served from 11:00 a.m-4:00p.m. They have a large assortment of burgers to choose from including Garden Burgers. Sandwiches include; French Dip, Hot Beef & Cheddar, Philly Steak, Veggie and Breaded Cod. Mexican items feature Burritos, Enchiladas, Tacos and Nachos.

All dinners at Steakhouse include your choice of Baked or Au Gratin Potato, Roll, Butter, Homemade Soup, Salad, and Dessert Bar. Entrees include; London Broil, Top Sirloin, Rib Eye Steaks, Bacon Wrapped Filet Mignon and Chicken Fried Steak. Other items are Teriyaki Chicken, Lemon Pepper Chicken, Southwestern Chicken and Pork Chops. It's complimented by childrens menu and a full bar.

CONTACT US

[970] 921-4386
356 Hwy. 92
Crawford, Colorado 81415

WHAT'S COOKING

American/Mexican

HOW TO GET HERE

Located in the center of
Crawford on Hwy. 92.

AREA ACTIVITIES

Fishing
Camping
Water Skiing
Swimming
Hunting
Hiking
Biking
Trail Riding

AREA INFORMATION

Crawford Colorado Chamber of Commerce
www.crawfordcountry.org

Crawford Colorado Tourist Attractions
www.planetware.com

Black Canyon of the Gunnison National Park
www.nps.gov/blca

Butch's Lobster Bar

Snowmass Village, Colorado

High above the Roaring Fork Valley, at the top of Snowmass Village in the Timberline Condos resides Butch's Lobster Bar. Butch's has been an Aspen and Snowmass favorite since 1979. It is truly an authentic East Coast Restaurant, as the owner is a former lobsterman from Cape Cod.

The appetizer list at Butch's is huge, it features; Steamed Shrimp in Scampi Butter, Shrimp Dijon, Garlic Shrimp, Coconut Shrimp, Steamed Clams or Clams Casino. They serve Fresh Oysters On The Half Shell, and Oysters Rockefeller, [Casino or Romanoff]. Add to that; Crab Cakes, Mussels, Calamari, Escargot, Smoked Salmon or Lobster Rolls and you have a great start to your meal.

Entrees at Butch's feature; Shrimp Scampi Italian, Shrimp Alfredo, the legendary Shannon's Shrimp, Linguini with Red or White Clam Sauce, or New York Steak. Or indulge in; Alaskan King Crab, Barbecued Ribs or of course, Live Maine Lobster. The Lobsters are available regular size or by the pound and are served steamed, grilled or broiled.

CONTACT US

[970] 923-4004
[970] 923-7311
264 Snowmelt Road
Snowmass Village, Colorado
81615
E-Mail: butch@sopris.net
Web Site: www.butchslobster.com

WHAT'S COOKING

East Coast Seafood

HOW TO GET HERE

Located at the Timberline Condos at the top of Snowmass Village or ask a local.

AREA ACTIVITIES

Skiing
Hiking
Biking
Rafting
Fishing
Kayaking
Cross Country Skiing
Climbing
Hut Trips

AREA INFORMATION

Snowmass Village
www.snowmassvillage.com

Snowmass Colorado
www.snowmassbookit.com

Aspen and Snowmass Village
www.aspensnowmass.com

Harmel's Ranch Resort

Almont, Colorado

Harmels Ranch Resort is located 8,400 feet high in the central Colorado Rockies. It is situated in the middle of the pristine Taylor River at the confluence of three rivers and surrounded by the Gunnison National Forest. In mining times, ore from camps in the area was brought to Almont to be transported via rail to Gunnison. When the railroad folded and the mining boom ended, people remained living in Almont's tranquil resort like setting. Rustic cabins still dot the landscape, and time seems to move a little slower in Almont.

Harmel's serves breakfast, lunch and dinner 7 days a week starting in mid May till the end of September. At breakfast you have a lot of great options. You can pick from Eggs Benedict, Eggs Florentine, Chicken Fried Steak or Biscuits and Gravy. Other options include creating your own omelet, indulging in the all you can eat Pancakes or French Toast or enjoying the Breakfast Buffet.

Lunch at Harmels can be enjoyed al-fresco on their beautiful decks overlooking the Taylor River and the surrounding Scenery.

Tuesday and Sunday evenings are Harmel's really big Smorgasbord nights. Thursdays they have their famous Chuck Wagon BBQ where Western Style Pork Ribs and Chicken are featured. Wednesday and Friday nights they offer a full service, four course, dining experience. On Mondays don't miss the Steak and Crab Cookout. Your table is waiting.

Dinner selection highlights are; Filet Mignon, New York Strip Steak, Tequila Chipotle Glazed Pork Loin, or Ribeyes. They also have; Lamb Chops, Jumbo Sea Scallops, Swordfish. Of course save room for delicious desserts.

CONTACT US

[970] 641-1740
[800] 235-3402
6748 County Road 742
P.O. Box 399
Almont, Colorado 81210
E-Mail: stay@harmels.com
Web Site: www.harmels.com

WHAT'S COOKING

American BBQ

HOW TO GET HERE

6 miles east of Almont on County Road 742

AREA ACTIVITIES

Fishing
Horseback Riding
Swimming
Hunting
Hiking
Climbing

AREA INFORMATION

Recreation And Travel Info
www.gunnisoncrestedbutte.com

Crested Butte Chamber
www.crestedbuttechamber.com

Mesa Lakes Resort

Mesa, Colorado

Mesa Lakes Resort and Beaver Lake Restaurant are one of the few remaining old fashioned resorts in the state of Colorado. Mesa Lakes Resort is located in the beautiful surroundings of the Grand Mesa National Forest, 45 miles east of Grand Junction on Highway 65. In 1996 the highway was designated a National Scenic Byway. Mesa Lakes elevation is at 9800 feet.

The Beaver Lake Restaurant serves breakfast, lunch and dinner all year. Breakfast is from 7a.m.-11a.m. and features; Biscuits & Gravy, Sausage, Bacon & Eggs, Hot Cakes, French Toast, Huevos de Mesa and some extraordinary homemade Cinnamon Rolls.

Lunch at Beaver Lake includes Hamburgers, Cheeseburgers, and Grilled Chickens sandwiches with soup, salad or chili. They also have BBQ Beef, BLT, Black Russian, Grilled Cheese and Rueben sandwiches.

The dinner selections are small but tasty with 2 sizes of Top Sirloins, Chicken Fried Steak and Spaghetti with Garlic Bread. Leave room for homemade pie.

CONTACT US

(970) 268-5467
251 Hwy. 65
P.O. Box 230
Mesa, Colorado 81643-0230

WHAT'S COOKING

American

HOW TO GET HERE

Located 50 miles east of Grand Junction on Hwy. 65, 5 miles east of Powderhorn Ski Area.

AREA ACTIVITIES

Skiing
Hiking
Fishing
Hunting
Cross Country Skiing
Horse Back Riding
Biking

AREA INFORMATION

Grand Mesa National Scenic Byway
www.grandmesabyway.org

Grand Mesa National Forest
gorp.away.com/gorp/resource/us

Grand Mesa National Forest Campgrounds
www.forestcamping.com

The Nordic Inn
Twin Lakes, Colorado

The Nordic Inn is located in the heart of the San Isabel National Forest at the base of Mt. Elbert, Colorado's highest peak in historic Twin Lakes.

Truly a historic inn and restaurant, the Nordic Inn has no TV's or phones in the rooms. There is a sitting room with videos, books and games for all to enjoy. Breakfast is included for all overnight guests. Dinners are served 7 nights a week from 4pm.-9pm. and lunches are served on the weekends

For starters, at the Nordic Inn, try Lamb Shepherd's Pie, served with a sage biscuit or Mushrooms Strudel, a crisp, savory pastry filled with mushroom duxelle. They also have Pizza Rustica, a thick, Ricotta pie with spinach, crab, and applewood smoked bacon, served with tomato basil cream, and Spinach and Smoked Trout Salad with walnuts, bleu cheese, artichoke hearts, and lavender champagne vinaigrette.

Entrees at the Nordic include; Flatiron Steaks with basil mashed potatoes, Southwestern Cordon Bleu, a version of the classic, with green chilies, crab and Wisconsin sharp cheddar, Rainbow Trout with herbed cranberry and stuffed with applewood smoked bacon, Beef Coulotte Steak with mushroom bordelaise sauce and Panzotti with smoked artichoke hearts, a traditional Italian Ravioli, stuffed with wild baby greens, walnuts and ricotta.

The Nordic Inn has 13 guest rooms and all have been romantically restored with featherbeds and antiques. During the gold and silver rush, over a hundred years ago, this was a bustling stop on the way to or from Aspen, as well as a base camp for local miners. The town is now home to less than 100 year-round residents.

CONTACT US

[719] 486-1830]
[800] 626-7812
6435 Hwy. 82
Twin Lakes, Colorado 81251
www.twinlakesnordiclodge.com
inf0@twinlakesnordiclodge.com

WHAT'S COOKING

Continental

HOW TO GET HERE

Located 30 miles east of Aspen on Hwy. 82 over Independence Pass.

AREA ACTIVITIES

Skiing
Hiking
Kayaking
Rafting
Boating
Fishing
Climbing
Biking
Camping

AREA INFORMATION

Twin Lakes, Colorado
www.fourteenernet.com/twinlakes

Leadville, Colorado
www.leadville.com

Twin Lakes, Hotels and Motels
www.metrotravelguide.com

The Paradox Grille
Gateway, Colorado

Gateway Canyons and the Paradox Grille is a new destination resort and world class car museum located in the spectacular red rock country of Western Colorado. Surrounded by majestic buttes, mesas and winding canyon roads the new resort features comfortable accommodations, innovative dining and outdoor adventures of all kind. Open year-round with gas, food and lodging.

The Paradox Grille's eclectic menu offers western, southwestern and traditional dishes that represent the best of Colorado cuisine. Go and enjoy breakfast, lunch, dinner or just a little something from their appetizer list. Relax and enjoy the views and ambience.

Breakfast favorites are; huevos rancheros, biscuits and gravy, steak and eggs, burritos, buttermilk griddle cakes and classic omelets.

For lunch at the Paradox Grille, try a black Angus or bison burger or the Cubano [slow cooked garlic pork roast, shaved ham, swiss cheese, dill pickles on a grilled baguette with smoky chipotle aioli]. Southwestern fare includes a variety of tacos such as carne asada, pollo asada, pescado, frijoles negros and carnitas.

Try something from the Grille's large appetizer list including stone-baked quesadillas, chili con queso, Ancho BBQ ribs, buffalo sopas, grilled shrimp cocktails, masa fried oyster shot or chile verde con puerco.

Dinner specials feature; porterhouse steaks, bone-in rib eye cowboy steak, Colorado lamb loin chops, rainbow trout, baked penne pasta or enchiladas, carne asada, pollo asado, and tostada de camarones asadas.

Thirsty? Check out the bar selections. Hand brewed Colorado beers, signature margaritas, their own fruit infused spirits and a great wine list.

CONTACT US

[866] 671-4733
43200 Hwy. 141
P.O. Box 319
Gateway, Colorado 81622
E-Mail: info@gtwycanyons.com
Web Site: gtwycanyons.com

WHAT'S COOKING

Western/Southwestern/
Continental

HOW TO GET HERE

Located 40 miles southwest of
Grand Junction on Hwy. 141

AREA ACTIVITIES

Running
Car Museum
Hiking
Biking
Hunting
4 Wheeling
Climbing
Skiing

AREA INFORMATION

Gateway, Colorado
Automobile Museum
gatewayautomuseum.com

Grand Junction Visitor Bureau
www.visitgrandjunction.com

Grand Junction, Colorado
ZWine Country
www.visitgrandjunction.com/
winecountryhtml

The Pine Creek Cookhouse

Ashcroft, Colorado

The Pine Creek Cookhouse serves exquisite meals in spectacular surroundings with breathtaking views of the Elk Mountain range.

Ashcroft and the upper Castle Creek Valley surrounding the Pine Creek Cookhouse are a veritable mecca of recreational opportunities. You can visit the historic Ghost Town of Ashcroft or hike up American and Cathedral trails to hidden pristine lakes. The rivers and beaver ponds of upper Castle Creek offer Gold Medal trout fishing and the flowers, wildlife and mountain scenery are a must see.

Originally built in 1971 and destroyed by fire in April 2003, the Pine Creek Cookhouse was spectacularly re-created as an authentic log cabin of native Colorado logs. In the winter, guests leave their cars behind at the historic Ghost Town of Ashcroft to cross country ski, snowshoe or ride by horse drawn sleigh to the Cook-house. In the summer you can drive or bike all the way to the restaurant.

Lunch highlights include; Smoked Trout, Lobster Spring Rolls, Spinach and Vegetarian Crepes and grilled Quail Salad. They also have Buffalo Rueben Sandwiches, Wild Game Sheep Stew and Herb Crusted Trout.

For dinner try Seared Foie Grois, Duck 3 ways with a trio of sauces, Jack Daniels Marinated Caribou, Wild King Salmon, Braised Lamb Shanks or Cervena Elk Tenderloin.

Thirsty? The Cookhouse has a full bar and a great wine list, so kick back on the deck and indulge in your favorite libation and enjoy the views.

CONTACT US

[970] 925-1044
Fax: [970] 925-7939
Mail: 314 South 2nd Street
Aspen, Colorado 81611
E-Mail: info@pinecreekcookhouse
www.pinecreekcookhouse.com

WHAT'S COOKING

Mountain Gourmet Cuisine

HOW TO GET HERE

Located 11 miles south of Aspen
on Castle Creek Road

AREA ACTIVITIES

Cross Country Skiing
Skiing
Hiking
Fishing
4 Wheeling
Climbing
Photography
Ghost Town

AREA INFORMATION

Ashcroft, Colorado Cross Country Skiing
roz.dudden.com/
ashcroft,pinecreek

Aspen and Snowmass Village
www.aspensnowmass.com

Aspen Chamber Resort Assn.
www.aspenpitkin.com

Poppies Bistro

Aspen, Colorado

Called by many the most romantic restaurant in Colorado, Poppies is located on the tranquil, westernmost edge of town, making it feel like a secret retreat, and the intimate atmosphere, loaded with Victorian charm, just begs you to play Casanova. The restaurant rambles through a series of small creaky rooms and the décor includes lovely paintings, antiques and lace curtains. It's cozy in the winter, but even better in the summer after an afternoon concert at the nearby music tent.

Aspen is a favorite Colorado ski resort; World renowned for its downhill skiing. It sits at the upper end of the Roaring Fork Valley, with the Roaring Fork River, a superb trout stream running through town. It offers an interesting history, challenging outdoor recreation opportunities, abundant cultural activities, pleasant climate and beautiful scenery.

Start your night at Poppies with a taste of one of their great appetizers. Choose from Lobster Relleno, Dungeness Crab Cakes, Tempura Fried Black Tiger Shrimp, Caesar Salad or Hudson Valley Foie Gras. Poppies also has a bar menu, and in the summer months you can eat outside and enjoy the great views of Aspen Mountain.

Entrees at Poppies feature; Steak au Poive, Batter Sautéed Rainbow Trout, Roasted One Half Chicken, Herbed Goat Cheese Ravioli, Maple Leaf Mahogany Duck, Roast Colorado Lamb Rack, Braised Pork on the Bone, Poppies Bouillabaisse and lots of Fresh Fish Specials. Favorite items; are Sesame Crusted Ahi, Grilled Buffalo Tenderloin and the best Steak au Poivre in the state. After dinner retire to their very cozy bar and enjoy a Port and Stilton after dinner treat while discussing which ski area you're going to enjoy the next day.

CONTACT US

[970] 925-2333
834 W. Hallam Street
Aspen, Colorado 81612

WHAT'S COOKING

Rustic Provencal with
a Colorado flair.

HOW TO GET HERE

At the western entrance to Aspen on Hwy. 82, cross the Castle Creek Bridge and Poppies will be on your left.

AREA ACTIVITIES

Skiing
Fishing
Mountain Biking
Rafting
Hiking
Jeeping
Golfing
Cross Country Skiing
Concerts
Swimming

AREA INFORMATION

Aspen and Snowmass Village
www.aspensnowmass.com

City of Aspen & Pitkin County
wwwaspitkin.com

Aspen Chamber Resort
www.aspenchamber.org

The Aspen Times
wwwaspenalive.com

The Red Rose Café

Palisade, Colorado

After 25 years of success on the front range, as the Rose Café, the restaurant was uprooted and moved to the western slope, at the foot of massive Mt. Garfield.

Located in the middle of Colorado's Wine Country, this quaint restaurant offers a surprising combination of Italian and Vietnamese cuisine and friendly conscientious service.

The Vietnamese side of the menu starts with appetizers such as; Vietnamese Egg Rolls, Spring Rolls and Vietnamese Chicken Salad. Entrees include; Oriental Pasta, an incredible selection of Rice Noodle Bowls with choices of Pork, Chicken, Shrimp or Beef. They also have Chinese or Temupura Catfish and Vietnamese Seafood Curry.

Italian selections from the Red Rose start with appetizers such as; Steamed Prince Edwards Mussels, Bruschetta, Calamari or Chicken Caesar and Shrimp Louie Salads. Entrees include; lots of different pastas, Meatball and Sausage, New Orleans [shrimp, scallops, mushrooms and artichokes in a Cajun cream sauce] and Lasagna. Other highlights on the menu are Chicken Marsala, Chicken Asiago, Mediterranean Salmon, Pork Chops and Black Jack New York Steak.

CONTACT US

[970] 464-7673
235 Main Street
Palisade, Colorado 81526

WHAT'S COOKING

Italian/Vietnamese

HOW TO GET HERE

Palisade is 10 miles east of Grand Junction . On I-70 East to exit 42, south 0.3 mi. turn left on 373 1 mile, turn right on main, Red Rose Will be on the left.

AREA ACTIVITIES

Wine Tours and Tastings
Fishing
Skiing
Golfing
Hunting
Hiking
Climbing

AREA INFORMATION

Palisade Chamber of Commerce
www.palisadecoc.com

Palisade Peach Festival
www.palisadepeachfest.com

Colorado Wine Fest
www.coloradowinefest.com

The Redstone Inn

Redstone, Colorado

An enchanting inn nestled on the banks of the sparkling Crystal River. This incredible 22 acre property is located in the town of Redstone and the historic Redstone Inn is the focal point of this 100 year old arts and crafts town. Located on the edge of the White River National Forest, Redstone is an outdoor enthusiast's paradise, and an aesthetic wonderland offering world class recreational activities and endless opportunities for adventure.

Don't forget to take a tour of the newly re-opened, world famous Redstone Castle just west of the Redstone Inn.

In the Dinning Room and South Veranda, dinners start at 5:30 and reservations are encouraged. To start your meal you might try the Elk in Phyllo Purse or the Shrimp, Crab & Avocado Martini from the appetizer list or any one of 5 different salads. Entrees include Roast Duck, Rocky Mountain Trout, Lamb Chops, New York Steaks, Chili Lime Grilled Shrimp or slow Roasted Prime Rib. The atmosphere and service at the Redstone Inn make for a memorable dining experience. After dinner get cozy around one of the huge fireplaces.

At the Grille & Patio, breakfast, lunch and dinner are served in the casual "English Tavern" ambiance overlooking the pool, with views of the Elk Mountain range. The Grilles menus are fun and affordable. The Grille offers snacks, appetizers, salads, sandwiches, pizza and a childrens menu. They also have specialty items including fresh Rocky Mountain Trout, Ribs, Carnitas, Fish & Chips, and Chicken Alfredo. For dinner they feature New York Steak, Pork Chops, Herb Chicken, Salmon and Prime Rib.

CONTACT US

[970] 963-2526
[800] 748-2524
Fax: [970] 963-2527
82 Redstone Blvd.
Redstone, Colorado 81623
E-Mail: info@redstoneinn.com
Web Site: www.redstoneinn.com

WHAT'S COOKING

Creative Continental

HOW TO GET HERE

From Carbondale Take Hwy.
133 south 18 miles. Turn Left

AREA ACTIVITIES

Hiking
Tennis
Horseback Riding
Fishing
Skiing
Pool
Sleigh Rides
Nordic Trails
Ice Climbing

AREA INFORMATION

Redstone
www,redstonecolorado.com

Aspen Chamber Resort Assn.
www.aspenchamber.org

Redstone Colorado
www.planet.com/colorado/
redstone-us

The Rivers Restaurant

Glenwood Springs, Colorado

Nestled in a beautiful mountainous valley on the western slope of Colorado in Glenwood Springs lies the Rivers Restaurant. The Rivers Restaurant has a classic, bright atmosphere, great creative menu offerings, and a deck that makes a great place to sip a cocktail while watching the boaters and fishermen below.

The Rivers has the most eclectic, yet affordable collection of the finest steaks, seafood, poultry, pasta and desserts in the Roaring Fork Valley. Start with a variety of appetizers such as; Trout Pate, Godzilla Shrimp, Baked Brie, Grilled Elk Quesadilla and Flash Fried Calamari and Rock Shrimp on a Jalapeno Lime Aioli.

Entrees include; Blackened Pork Medallions, Citrus Crusted Salmon, New York Steak, Filet Mignon, Wild Boar and Mushrooms Ragout. In addition they have; Prime Rib, Medallions of Elk, Shrimp and Veal Françoise and Jumbo Scallops and Shrimp in a Spicy Oriental Chili Sauce. The Rivers has a full bar and a huge wine list as well as lots of great scotches.

CONTACT US

[970] 928-8813
2525 Grand Ave.
Glenwood Springs, Colorado
81601
Web Site: the riversrestaurant.com

WHAT'S COOKING

Continental

HOW TO GET HERE

I-70, to the Glenwood Springs exit and head south down Grand Ave. at 27th Street turn right [west] and go 1 block and turn right.

AREA ACTIVITIES

Biking
Camping
Fishing
Four Wheeling
Cavern Tours
Golf/ Mini Golf
Hot Springs Pool
Hiking
Skiing

AREA INFORMATION

City of Glenwood Springs
www.ciglenwoodsprings.co.us

Glenwood Springs Chamber Resort
wwwglenwoodchamber.com

Spruce Lodge
Grand Mesa, Colorado

Sitting high on top of Grand Mesa, the largest flat top mountain in the world, The Spruce Lodge is surrounded by over 300 lakes and 360,000 plus acres of United States Forest Service land. Truly a fisherman's paradise, it is home to miles of recreational trails. From a vista near the Lodge, one can view five different mountain ranges, the impressive Black Canyon and three river valleys. Visit this gem and enjoy fine cuisine and a full bar amid the rustic elegance of Spruce Lodge.

Spruce Lodge serves breakfast, lunch and dinner in the rustic elegance of their dining room. Breakfast is served from 9:00 to 11:30 and features Buttermilk Pancakes, Steak and Eggs, Omelets and Biscuits and Gravy.

Lunch includes; Hamburgers, a citrus marinated Chicken Wrap, Fish and Chips, Paninis , Pastas and Salads.

Favorite dinner entrees include; Prime Rib Roast, Tenderloin served with Bordelaise Sauce, Rib Eye and New York Steaks. Additional specialties are; Lemon Garlic Chicken, Fish & Chips, Salmon, Catfish, Chicken Mascarpone, Caesar and Oriental Chicken Salads. The Spruce Lodge also has a full bar and a great wine list.

CONTACT US

[970] 856-6240
[800] 850-7221
20658 Baron Lake Drive
Cedaredge, Colorado 81413
E-Mail: sprucelodgegm@aol.com
Web Site: www.sprucelodge.com

WHAT'S COOKING

American

HOW TO GET HERE

16 miles N of Cedaredge on Hwy. 65. From Hwy. 65 turn at the Grand Mesa Visitor Center and go 1 mile.

AREA ACTIVITIES

4 Wheeling
Skiing
Fishing
Hunting
Nordic Trails
Hiking

AREA INFORMATION

Grand Mesa Scenic Byways
www.grandmesabyway.org

Cedaredge Area Chamber of Commerce

The Grill Bar & Café

Leadville, Colorado

The Grill Bar & Café is located in Leadville, North America's highest incorporated city at a lofty perch of 10,430 feet. The legendary frontier mining town features seventy square blocks of Victorian architecture.

The Grill has been continuously operating as a food & drink establishment since 1938 and has a very colorful history. Come visit and learn about the rowdy past tales while sipping on signature margaritas and enjoying the views of Colorado's two highest mountains, Mount Massive and Mount Elbert.

The Grill Bar & Café serves dinner daily starting at 4:00p.m. It also serves lunch on the weekends in the summer with incredible views from their outside deck and gardens. The original watercolors by Linda Duthie throughout the restaurant are for sale. It's like a gallery, feel free to browse.

Favorites on the dinner menu at the Grill include; Enchiladas, Tacos, Vegetarian Plates, Tamales, Rellenos and all different combinations of each. Specialties feature Huevos Rancheros, Corn Tortilla Flautas, Beef Chicken or Shrimp Fajitas, Stuffed Sopapillas and Sopapillas Especiales. For dessert try; Cinnamon, Strawberry or Banana Sopapillas, or a Banana Taco with Chocolate Ice Cream or Hot Apple Pie Ala Mode with a Brandy Butter Sauce. The Grill also has a full bar featuring a large variety of unique tequilas and the best margaritas in the west.

CONTACT US

[719] 486-9930
Fax: [719] 486-5063
Web Site: www.grillbarcafe.com
715 Elm Street
Leadville, Colorado 80461

WHAT'S COOKING

Mexican

HOW TO GET HERE

From the north, go through Leadville south on U.S. 24, turn right on Jackson Road. Jackson Road becomes Elm.

AREA ACTIVITIES

Rafting
Hiking
Biking
Golfing
Skiing
Museums
4 Wheeling
Fishing

AREA INFORMATION

Leadville
www.leadville.com

Leadville and Lake County
Chamber of Commerce
www.leadvilleusa.com

White Buffalo West
Battlement Mesa, Colorado

High above the Colorado River in Western Colorado and at the base of the beautiful Grand Mesa National Forest, sits the White Buffalo West Restaurant. The White Buffalo is renowned for its legendary food and sacred spirits. Situated above the Colorado River with high desert mountain views of the Battlements and the Bookcliffs, Battlement Mesa is a unique community with magnificent scenery.

The White Buffalo serves lunch and dinner7 days a week. For lunch pick from a large selection of salads, sandwiches, and burgers.

At dinner start with appetizers such as; Nachos, Chicken Wings, Crab and Artichoke Dip, Rocky Mountain Oysters, or Southwestern Egg Rolls.

Dinner highlights include; Rib Eye Steak, Filet Mignon, Porterhouse Pork Chop, Grilled Salmon and Shrimp Primavera. Also try the Pork Osso Bucco and the Prime Rib.

The sports bar at the White Buffalo has ten wide screen TV's and an atmosphere that reminds you of a Vegas Sports Book. With nine draft beers and a huge old fashioned back bar with over 225 different bottles, nearly any drink can be made. DJ music plays Wednesday, Friday and Saturday, and in the summer the patio opens, which has its own bar.

CONTACT US
[970] 285-1680
73 Sippelle Drive Ste. A
Battlement Mesa, Colorado
81635-9213

WHAT'S COOKING
American

HOW TO GET HERE
Take I-70 Exit 75 Battlement Mesa. Turn north on Battlement Parkway for 1.6 miles, turn right on Spencer Parkway for 0.8 miles and turn left on Sippelle Drive.

AREA ACTIVITIES
Hunting
Fishing
Rafting
Golfing
Tennis
Skiing
Snowmobiling

AREA INFORMATION
Battlement Mesa Company
www.battlemesa.com

Battlement Mesa
www.battlementmesacolorado.com

Woody Creek Tavern

Woody Creek, Colorado

The Woody Creek Tavern is located in the heart of the Rocky Mountains adjacent to the Hunter/Fryingpan Wilderness Area. The Tavern is the sort of rustic hangout one might find in small Colorado towns, and is the insider hot spot in Aspen for locals and celebrities. The place is known for the pig on the roof and its eclectic wall hangings. The Tavern was the favorite hangout of the late gonzo author Hunter S. Thompson.

The Woody Creek Taverns menu offers soups, salads, sandwiches and Mexican grub, and their great funky décor and awesome summertime patio will win you over.

At the Tavern try some of the appetizers that will keep you coming back; Smoked Salmon, Smoked Trout, Flautas and Chicken Wings.

Dinners at Woody Creek start at 5:30 p.m. They are open 7 nights a week. Selections include; Limousin New York Steak [Limousin beef is lower in cholesterol and calories], or Blackened New York's, BBQ Pork Porterhouse, BBQ Chicken and Oven Roasted Chicken. On the Southwestern side of the menu they have; Fresh Tilapia Tacos, Vegan Tacos, Chicken Enchiladas, Pork Tamales Vegetarian Tamales and Black Bean Burritos.

The Woody Creek Tavern's bar features fresh squeezed lime margaritas made with top shelve Herradura Blanco, 100% Blue Agave. They are so strong they are not sold by the pitcher. Wines by the glass and bottle are available, including Woody Creek Cellars award winning Merlot. There are plenty of cold beers available with the Flying Dog Brew Pubs Doggie Style Amber on tap.

CONTACT US

[970] 923-4585
002 Woody Creek Plaza
Woody Creek, Colorado 81656

WHAT'S COOKING

American/ Southwestern

HOW TO GET HERE

North of Aspen on Hwy. 82, 8 miles. Woody creek exit, go down hill turn left at y and go 1/2 miles.

AREA ACTIVITIES

Scenic/ Historic Byways
Kayaking
Rafting
Biking Trails
Fishing
Skiing
Snowmobiling

AREA INFORMATION

Aspen and Snowmass Village
www.aspensnowmass.com

Aspen Chamber Resort Association
www.aspenchamber.org

Woody Creek Area Guide
woodycreekco.areaguides.net

HONEY

THE WOODY CREEK STORE AND GALLERY
GALLERY

Southern Colorado

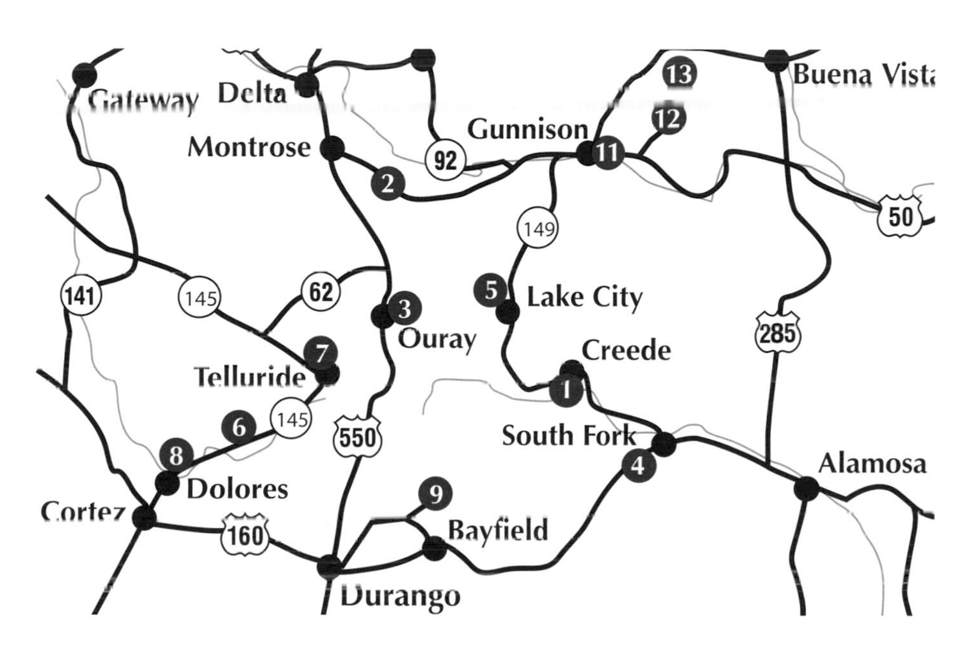

The Antlers Rio Grande Lodge & Riverside Restaurant

Creede, Colorado

An unbelievable jewel about 5 miles west of Creede, Colorado on an incredible pristine 70 acres along the Rio Grande River. The Antlers has continuously operated as a guest ranch for over 100 years. The Antlers and the Riverside Restaurant are open May through September and offer cabins, rooms and RV sites. The quaint Victorian mining town of Creede is only 5 miles away, with restaurants, shops, and the best repertory theater in the west.

Homesteaded in 1896, the Antlers Rio Grande Lodge is a picturesque mountain retreat nestled between the banks of the Rio Grande River and Silver Thread Scenic Byway.

Amenities at the Antlers include a gift and sundries shop, pool table, game and card tables, hot tub, private fishing, hayrides, campfires, petting farm and guest horse corrals.

Appetizers at the Riverside Restaurant start with; Lobster Bisque soup and Maryland Lump Blue Crab Cakes. The restaurants specialties are; Pork Tenderloin wrapped in Apple Wood Smoked Bacon, Oven Roasted Rack of Lamb, Spiced Filet of Salmon and Herb Marinated Elk Loin. The Riversides desserts feature; Key Lime Pie, scrumptious Chocolate Cake and Bananas Foster Pie.

CONTACT US
[719] 658-2423
26222 Highway 149
Creede, Colorado 81130
Web Site: www.antlerslodge.com

WHAT'S COOKING
Continental Riverside Dining

HOW TO GET HERE
5 miles west of Creede, on Hwy. 149 near milepost 26

AREA ACTIVITIES
Fishing
Hunting
Rafting
4 Wheeling
Trail Biking
Hiking
Golfing
Repertory Theater

AREA INFORMATION
City of Creede
www.creede.com

Creede. Colorado Ghost Town
www.ghosttowns.com

Creede Colorado Lodging
www.fourteenernet.com

The Inn At Arrowhead

Arrowhead, Colorado

A friendly lodge, restaurant and lounge located high in the Colorado Rockies. The Houseman family and its friendly staff invite you to enjoy their hospitality at the Inn At Arrowhead. Nestled amidst aspen and spruce groves at about 9,300 feet elevation, the Inn offers all the seclusion or activity you desire.

The Inn has twelve rooms and a honeymoon suite. All rooms have plush carpeting, cozy comforters, bathrooms with showers and your own private fireplace. There is also a hot tub on the second deck with great views, music and an Irish Pub and Restaurant.

The Inn serves Breakfast, Lunch and Dinner in their cozy restaurant with all the beautiful fireplaces. Breakfast is traditional English style with eggs, sausage, bacon, baked beans, tomatoes, French Toast, omelets and coffee and tea. Lunch includes burgers and lots of homemade sandwiches and salads.

The dinner menu changes often but entrees usually include a specially-created pasta, great steaks, terrific chicken creations, or their widely-acclaimed seafood entrees. Of course on Saturday nights they offer their famous prime rib dinners.

In the lounge, enjoy your favorite mixed drink, or choose from a variety of beers and fine wines. Sit around the fireplaces and share tall tales about your outdoor adventures with other guests, or enhance the size of that fish you caught.

CONTACT US
[970] 862-8206
E-Mail: info@arrowheadinn.net
Web Site: www.arrowheadinn.net
21401 Alpine Plateau Road
Cimmaron, Colorado 81220

WHAT'S COOKING
Irish Pub Food

HOW TO GET HERE
Halfway between Gunnison and Montrose on Hwy. 50, turn south on Alpine Plateau Road for 5 ½ miles.

AREA ACTIVITIES
Hiking
Horse Back Riding
Mountain Bike Trails
Fishing
Boating
Snowmobiling
Cross Country Skiing
Alpine Skiing

AREA INFORMATION
San Juan National Forest
www.fs.us/r2/sanjuan

Black Canyon of the Gunnison National Park
www.nps.gov/blca

Blue Mesa Reservoir
www.bluemesares.com

Bachelor-Syracuse Mine & The Miners Outdoor Café

Ouray, Colorado

Sitting high above Ouray, Colorado in the Uncompahgre National Forest the Bachelor Syracuse Mine features mine tours and Texas Bar-B-Q from May thru September. The mine tour takes visitors on a guided tram ride 3,350 feet into Gold Hill, a silver and gold mine. You will see the rich ore veins, work areas, and equipment used in mining. Gold panning and a visit to the turn-of-the-century Blacksmith shop and the Miners Outdoor Café are other highlights.

The Bachelor Syracuse serves an all you can eat breakfast from 8-12 and their BBQ lunch menu all day from 9am.-3pm. The all you can eat Breakfast includes; Omelets, Bacon, Sausage, Ham, Biscuits and Gravy, Chicken Fried Steak and Pork Chops. All meals are served al fresco in their outdoor café.

Lunch highlights at the Outdoor Café include; Burgers and Hot Dogs, Fried Catfish, Fried Chicken, Pork Chops, and of course BBQ, Beef, Sausage or Ham. Sides include Homemade Bread, Bar-B-Q Beans, Potato Salad, Coleslaw, French Fries, Sausage and Ham.

The Bachelor Mine is not a broken down abandoned mine, but rather a real silver and gold mine. It is well lighted, clean and has excellent natural ventilation. After your mine tour you can look forward to the great outdoor Al Fresco dining at the Miners Outdoor Café.

CONTACT US

[970] 325-0220
[800] 222-8545
Fax: [970] 325-4500
1222 County Road 14
Ouray, Co. 81427
E-Mail: minetour@gwe.net
www.bachelorsyracuse.com

WHAT'S COOKING

Texas B-B-Q

HOW TO GET HERE

1 mile north of Ouray on Hwy. 550, then 1 mile east on CR14

AREA ACTIVITIES

Hiking
Swimming
Ice Climbing
Golfing
4 Wheeling
Skiing
Gold Panning

AREA INFORMATION

Ouray Visitor Guide
www.ouraycolorado.com

City Of Ouray-Switzerland of America
www.ci.ouray.co.us

History Of Ouray, Colorado
www.narrsowgauge.org

The Chalet Swiss

South Fork, Colorado

The Chalet Swiss is a fabulous Swiss Restaurant in the high alpine mountains of southwestern Colorado. A truly wonderful place to enjoy the various foods from Switzerland. Focusing on fine dining, the Chalet Swiss provides a cozy ambiance and many opportunities to spoil your taste buds.

The bar at Chalet Swiss is always a great place to get started. They offer full bar service and a great selection of cold beers. Chalet Swiss has the valley's largest and well balanced wine list. In the summertime enjoy life on their beautiful outside deck with great views of the South Fork Valley. Lunch at Chalet Swiss includes soups and salads, burgers, fresh trout as well as buendnerteller, schnitzel, raclette and bratwurst.

Dinners begin with appetizers such as; Lobster and Fish Vol-Au-Vent, Maryland Crab Cakes, Escargots, or a large Shrimp Cocktail.Steak or Meat entrees include; Colorado Lamb Chops, New York Strip, Duck Breast A L'Orange and a Sirloin Steak. Seafood entrees are varied with; Sea Bass with Bay Scallops, Shrimp and Scallops, Trout Filets with White Wine Dill Sauce, and Halibut in Coconut Sauce with Curry. Swiss items are very interesting with a traditional Swiss Cheese Fondue and Swiss Raclette served family style. Other Swiss items are; Schnitzel, Cordon Bleu, Jaegerschnitzel, Zurich Geschnetzeltes, and Veal and Pork Bratwurst on the grill.

CONTACT US

[719] 873-1100
E-Mail: fredi@fone.net
Web Site: www.chaletswiss.com
31519 West Hwy. 160
South Fork, Colorado 81154

WHAT'S COOKING

Gourmet Swiss Cuisine

HOW TO GET HERE

Located on the western end of South Fork on Hwy. 160.

AREA ACTIVITIES

Skiing
Snowmobiling
Rafting
Golfing
Museums
4 Wheeling
Biking
Camping
Fishing
Hunting

AREA INFORMATION

Silver Thread Visitors Center
www.southfork.org

South Fork Chamber of Commerce
www.southforkcolorado.org

South Fork Campgrounds
www.southforkcampground.com

Crystal Lodge & Restaurant

Lake City, Colorado

Located in the remote southwestern San Juan Mountains, The Crystal Lodge & Restaurant has been a favorite since 1952. Surrounded by majestic pines, aspen and spruce the lodge provides suites and cabins for a great getaway.

Lake City was one of the most isolated major 19th century Colorado silver camps. On the east side of the San Juans, Lake City is the seat of Hinsdale County, the least populated county in the state. Prospecting began in the area around 1871, with good claims throughout the region. Four miles south of Lake City is San Cristobel, the second largest natural lake in Colorado.

The Crystal Lodge is open from late May to Late September for breakfast, dinner and take out picnic lunches. They also serve an extravagant Sunday Brunch. Dinner at the Crystal Restaurant starts with soup or two choices of salads. The house soup is "Southern Gumbo" [spicy gumbo with chicken, sausage, shrimp and crab.] The salad choices are; the house dinner salad with mixed greens and fresh vegetables, or the Caesar Salad with crisp romaine, crunchy croutons, creamy Caesar dressing and your choice of either chicken or shrimp.

Dinner entrees at the Crystal Lodge feature; New Zealand Rack of Lamb, Grilled Tenderloin Filet, Jerk Pork Tenderloin, Grilled Rib Eye and a Frenched Pork Chop. Fish and Fowl on the menu include; Seared Duck Breast, Pecan Crusted Chicken Breast, Cedar Planked Salmon [served on a hot cedar plank], Ruby Red Trout and Sesame Crusted Ahi Tuna. Desserts include; Turtle Fudge Cake, Key Lime Pie, 7 Layer Pie and Strawberries Romanoff.

CONTACT US

[970] 944-2201
[877] Go-Lodge
2175 Highway 149 South
Lake City, Colorado 81235
E-Mail: www.crystallodge.net
Web Site: www.crystallodge.net

WHAT'S COOKING

Gourmet Mountain Cuisine

HOW TO GET HERE

55 miles south of Gunnison on Hwy. 149 to Lake City. Go 2 miles south of Lake City on 149

AREA ACTIVITIES

Fishing
Mountain Biking
Boating on Lake Cristobal
Rafting
Horseback Riding
Miniature Golf
Jeeping
Musical and Theatrical Productions

AREA INFORMATION

Lake City History Weather & Shopping
www.lakecity.com

Lake City Visitor Guide
www.hinsdale-county.com

Dunton Hot Springs
Dunton, Colorado

Dunton Hot Springs is a ghost town so lovingly restored, so honestly weathered, nestled beneath the glistening snow fields of the San Juan peaks. The perfectly restored ghost town includes log cabins exquisitely furnished, a saloon serving food of startling quality, long trails followed by pampering massages and sensuous hot springs beneath shimmering snow banks.

Legend has it that in the old days Butch Cassidy and the Sundance Kid hid out in Dunton on numerous occasions. So, belly up to the authentic 100 year old bar with old time cowboy names etched in it including what seems to be Butch's and Sundance's signatures.

Everybody eats at one of their long tables, but that doesn't mean that they will not meet your dietary concerns and needs. They even pack up the most wonderful picnics for your fishing or horse expeditions.

Dunton's chefs use everything they grow either at their farm or in their vineyard. They also use local organic farmers markets and a food network that gathers food from every corner of Colorado. At various times of the year they use the mountain bounty of wild mushrooms, chanterelles, and boletos. These high standards of purchasing tell you precisely the kitchens priorities. Because of this, the menu changes daily. The chefs motto is, "cook it as carefully as possible and serve it as elegantly as you are able."

CONTACT US

[970] 882-4800
Fax: [970] 882-7474
P.O. Box 818
Dolores, Colorado 81323
info@duntonhotsprings.com
www.duntonhotsprings.com

WHAT'S COOKING

Continental

HOW TO GET HERE

Located on West Dolores Road, off Hwy. 145, between Telluride and Cortez.

AREA ACTIVITIES

Heli-Skiing
Hot Springs
Fly Fishing
Equestrian Adventures
Horseback Riding
Golfing
Hiking
Boxing
Yoga

AREA INFORMATION

Dolores Chamber of Commerce
doloreschamber.com

Dolores Chamber Tourism Info.
www.doloreschamber.com

Elk Mountain Resort

Telluride, Colorado

Elk Mountain Resort, is a spectacular new resort nestled in the heart of Colorado's San Juan Mountains, just 40 minutes from Telluride. With just over 275 sprawling acres and surrounded by pristine National Forests, Elk Mountain Resort is an oasis of natural beauty, accommodations, world class cuisine and an endless array of outdoor adventures.

The Tarragon Restaurant at Elk Mountain is a world class restaurant serving a tantalizing array of regional and Alpine Pyrenees cuisine.

The Tarragon Restaurant serves breakfast, lunch and dinner. Special items at breakfast are; Spanish Frittatas, Soufflé style Pancakes, Brioche French Toast and House Smoked Salmon. Specialty items at lunch include; Elk Mountain Burgers, Bison Burgers, Sun Dried Tomato Pesto Club Sandwiches and a Baby Lettuce Salad with Roasted Pears, Beets and Toasted Almonds.

Dinner at the Tarragon starts with appetizers such as Seared Sea Scallops with a Pomegranate and Lemon Caper Vinaigrette, or Smoked Pheasant Crepes in Madeira Cream with a Port Wine Reduction. Specialties of the house include; Braised Kobe Short Ribs with White Truffle Scented Mashers, Filet Mignon with Wild Mushrooms and Cabernet Demi-Glace, Seared Ahi Tuna with Toasted Fennel Crust and Sun Dried Tomato Couscous, Free Range Chicken Breast atop Bucatini Pasta or Grilled Rack of Lamb with Goat Cheese Polenta and Port Wine Demi-Glaze.

CONTACT US

[970] 252-4900
[877] 355-9255
[877] elkwalk
97 Elk Walk
Montrose, Colorado 81401
E-Mail: info@elkmountain.com
www.elkmountainresort.com

WHAT'S COOKING

Regional and Alpine Pyrenees

HOW TO GET HERE

Located 18.5 miles southwest of Montrose on Dave Wood Road

AREA ACTIVITIES

Horseback Riding
Rock Climbing
Jeep Tours
Mountain Biking
Hayrides & Sleigh Rides
High Ropes Course
Trap, Skeet & Five Stand Shooting
Cross Country Skiing
Ice Skating

AREA INFORMATION

Montrose Chamber of Commerce
wwwmontrosechamber.com

Telluride Visitors Guide
www.telluride.com

Town of Telluride
www.town.telluride.co.us

The Old Germany Restaurant

Dolores, Colorado

The Old Germany Restaurant is southwest Colorado's most unique and authentic German restaurant. It is located in a historic house built in 1908 in the beautiful Dolores River Canyon. It's surrounded by the Mount Wilson Primitive Area and the San Juan Rio Grande National Forest.

Dolores is home to the Anasazi Heritage Center, a unique federal museum, research center and curation facility. The center is not only a museum, it also houses more than 3 million artifacts and archives excavated from public lands in southwestern Colorado. Dolores is also headquarters for the new Canyons of the Ancients National Monument.

With the Dolores River running through town and mountains on both sides of the valley, Dolores is one of the truly unique vacation spots in Colorado. With gold medal fly fishing and spectacular scenery, Dolores and the Old Germany Restaurant are a must see.

The Old Germany offers Bavarian specialties. homemade desserts and German beers and wines. Their specialties include; Bratwurst, Knackwurst, Kasseler [smoked ribs with sauerkraut] and Wiener Schnitzel. Also great picks are Jagerbraten [pork roast in mushroom sauce], Sauerbraten [marinated roast] and New York Strip Steak.

The chefs at the restaurant grow their own their own sour cherries, strawberries, raspberries and fresh herbs. With that knowledge you might want to finish your meal with dessert. Suggestions include; Apple Strudel, a choice of Bavarian creams, a Chocolate Cream Torte and a wonderful Black Forest Cake.

In the warmer months the Old Germany Restaurant opens its outdoor Bavarian Beer Garden, featuring many great beers and wines.

CONTACT US

(970) 882-7519
200 S. 8th Street
Dolores, Colorado 81323
www.theoldgermanyrestaurant.com

WHAT'S COOKING

Authentic German Cuisine

HOW TO GET HERE

Dolores is halfway between Durango and Telluride on Hwy. 145 and the Restaurant is in the middle of town on the south side.

AREA ACTIVITIES

Hunting
Fishing/Boating
Camping
Hiking
Biking
National Parks and Monuments
Anasazi Heritage Center

AREA INFORMATION

Dolores Chamber of Commerce
doloreschamber.com

Dolores Chamber Tourism
www.doloreschamber.com/pages/info.htm

Mesa Verde Country
www.swcolor.org/tourism/dolores.html

Virginia's Steakhouse

Vallecito Lake, Colorado

In the heart of the unspoiled wilderness near beautiful Vallecito Lake resides Virginia's Steak House, serving great cuisine to the four corners area of Colorado for over 25 years.

Vallecito Lake is one of Colorado's largest and most beautiful lakes. The lake is surrounded by the San Juan National Forest and near the Weminuche Wilderness with wonderful trails to explore.

Virginia's Steakhouse has four dining rooms and they are all adorned with fireplaces, antique furniture, big game trophies, southwestern art originals, and plenty of wood paneling.

Virginia's only serves dinner and their menu is huge. Start with Appetizers like; Rocky Mountain Oysters, Jalapeno Poppers, Potato Skins, French Onion Soup, Sautéed Mushrooms, Jumbo Shrimp Cocktail and Rock Shrimp in Beer.

Entrees include; Salmon Oscar, Shrimp Scampi, Alaskan King Crab Legs and Australian Lobster Tail. Beef is featured also on Virginia's menu with New York Sirloin, Filet Mignon, Rib Eye, Top Sirloin, Prime Rib, Peppered Rib Eye and Teriyaki Sirloin to chose from. Specialties feature; Chicken fried Steak, Baby Back Pork Ribs, Smoked Brisket, Fried Chicken, Veal Marsala and Beef Stroganoff.

Virginia's also has a full bar with great selections of beers and wines. They have rooms and private cabins to rent, a live trout pond, volleyball courts and horseshoe pits.

CONTACT US

[970] 884-9495
Fax: [970] 884-9845
18044 County Road 501
Vallecito, Colorado 81122
E-Mail: steve@virginislodge.com
www.virginiaslodge.com

WHAT'S COOKING

American Steakhouse

HOW TO GET HERE

From Durango take Hwy. 160 east & drive 18.7 miles from the intersection of Hwy. 160 and 550. Turn left on CR 501 and drive 7.9 miles to intersection at CR 240. Stay right to remain on CR 501 and continue 10.6 miles to Virginia's Lodge.

AREA ACTIVITIES

Backpacking
Boating
Canoeing
Cross Country Skiing
Camping
Ice Fishing
Jet Skiing

AREA INFORMATION

Vacation Activities at Vallecito Lake
www.vallecitolakechamber.com

Vallecito Lake Chamber of Commerce
www.vallecitolake

The Wit's End Guest Ranch

Vallecito Lake, Colorado

The Wit's End is located in the beautiful Vallecito Lake Valley, surrounded by 12,000 and 14,000 foot granite peaks. This 133 year old renovated barn houses the restaurant and The Old Lodge At The Lake. The barn is constructed of rock and log, a genuine hand hewn building, three stories of old world charm and class.

One of the most spectacular and exclusive dude ranches in Colorado, the Wit's End is known throughout the world as a guest ranch of country elegance, unparalleled ambiance and exquisite accommodations. The resort is opened year round with fishing year round, and hunting from August to November..

Dining takes place in the Wit's End elegant "Old Lodge at the Lake" loaded with ambience and fine décor. The management and staff go to great lengths to provide an exquisitely detailed dining experience.

The dinner menus vary from Classic French to Classic Western BBQ. Some of the most popular BBQ items are Smoked Brisket of Beef, huge Roasts of Beef slowly turned on an open flame spit, grilled fresh Rocky Mountain Trout and deep fried Walleye.

Classic French favorites include; Baked Brie Encrute, Pan Fried Chicken Breast, Paella with Mussels, Clams, Shrimp, Crab and Lobster, or Prime Rib with Bordelaise and Béarnaise sauce. For dessert try the Poached Pear in Praline Basket with Wild berry Coulet.

They have nightly entertainment in the Crystal Tavern Lounge with a variety of wines, liqueurs and other alcoholic beverages.

CONTACT US

[800] 236-9483
[970] 884-4133
Fax: [970] 884-3261
354 County Road 500
Vallcito Lake, Colorado
Web Site: wwwwitsendranch.com

WHAT'S COOKING

Classic French/Classic BBQ

HOW TO GET HERE

From Durango take Hwy. 160 east and drive 18.7 miles from the intersection of Hwy. 160 & 550 to County Road 501. Turn left on Cr 501 and drive 7.9 miles to intersection at CR 240. Stay right to remain on CR 501 and continue 12.6 miles to Wits End.

AREA ACTIVITIES

Horseback Riding
Pontoon Boats
Fly Fishing
Float Trips
Sail Boating
Tennis
Pack Trips
Skiing
Golfing

AREA INFORMATION

Vallecito Lake Colorado
www.durango.org

Vallecito Chamber of Commerce
www.vallicitolakechamber.com

Pappy's On The Lake

Gunnison, Colorado

Sitting at 7500 feet high in the Curecanti National Recreation Area, Pappy's is a great place for a casual lunch or dinner in a relaxing atmosphere with a great view of Blue Mesa Reservoir. Pappy's is part of the Elk Creek Marina which includes slip rentals, boat rentals, a store and gift shop and boat repair facilities.

Blue Mesa Reservoir is Colorado's largest body of water, and has the largest Kokanee Salmon Fishery in the U.S. This 26 mile long lake offers all kinds of fishing opportunities.

Pappy's is open 7 days a week from Mothers Day until Labor Day. The menu starts with clam strips, chicken strips, mushroom caps and nachos. They have multiple salads including; Chefs, Caesar and Caesar with Salmon. There is a large selection of sandwiches including; Turkey, Italian Deli, Southwestern Chicken and Vegetarian. Additionally, Pappy's serves; Crab Cakes, Fried Shrimp and Fish and Chips.

Don't forget the; has Hamburgers, Buffalo Burgers, Chicken Breast Sandwiches and Salmon Sandwiches. For dessert try their; Ice Cream Sundaes, Cheese Cake, Chocolate Fudge Cake or Carrot Cake. Pappy's has a full liquor license and features; domestic, imports and micro brew beers, wines by the glass, margaritas and bloody marys.

CONTACT US
[970] 641-0403
24830 W. US Hwy. 50
P.O. Box 918
Gunnison, Colorado 81230

WHAT'S COOKING
American

HOW TO GET HERE
15 miles west of Gunnison
on Hwy. 50

AREA ACTIVITIES
Fishing
Skiing
Mountain Biking
Horseback Riding
Golfing
Nordic Skiing
Hunting
Camping
Boating
Water Skiing

AREA INFORMATION
Blue Mesa Reservoir
www.bluemesares.com

Gunnison Chamber of Commerce
www.gunnison.co.com

Visit Gunnison
www.visitgunnison.com

The Road Kill Café

Pitkin, Colorado

Located on the western side of the Rockies, high in the Sawatch Mountain Range at 9,000 feet, The Road Kill Cafes Motto is " you kill it we grill it". Pitkin is home to about 80 year round residents living among a cluster of log cabins, rusted antique cars and abandoned mine buildings. While visiting the Road Kill Café check out the museum and the turn of the century hotel. Many believe it is haunted and it was at one time considered the most modern in Colorado.

The Road Kill Café and Pitkin General Store serve breakfast, lunch and dinner every day except Saturday from Memorial Day to mid October. Start off breakfast at the Road Kill with; regular eggs, bacon, sausage and hash browns. Or try the; biscuits & gravy, pancakes, French toast, mountain miner muffins and breakfast burritos.

Lunch and dinners at the Road Kill Café include; hamburgers, chicken burgers, veggie burgers, hot dogs, pizza, nachos, home made burritos and tacos. Don't forget a soft drink, milk shakes or hand dipped ice cream cone.

Leave time to wander through the museum, and other attractions around Pitkin or drive over the Cumberland pass to the ghost town of Tin Cup.

CONTACT US
101 5th Avenue
Pitkin, Colorado 81241
(970) 641-7079

WHAT'S COOKING
American

HOW TO GET HERE
Go 9 miles east of Gunnison on Hwy. 50, turn north on County Road 209 for 25miles to Pitkin.

AREA ACTIVITIES
Hunting
Fishing
Hiking
Biking
4 Wheeling
Museums
Photography

AREA INFORMATION
Pitkin, Colorado
www.pitkincolorado.com

Gunnison Country Chamber
www.gunnison-co.com

City Of Gunnison
www.cityofgunnison-co.gov

Frenchy's On The Pond

Tin Cup, Colorado

High in the Gunnison National Forest at the foot of Cumberland Pass lies the town of Tin Cup and Frenchy's On The Pond Restaurant. Frenchy's is a small log cabin restaurant with a colorful past, where you can enjoy a great breakfast or lunch with a stunning view of the Cumberland Pass valley. The historic 150 year old restored ghost town of Tin Cup is a breath of fresh air, photogenic, pastoral, and the "get away from everything" kind of place that's so fun to find.

Frenchy's serves breakfast and lunch 7 days a week in the summer months only. The breakfast is fairly limited but the portions are large. Choices are ham, bacon, sausage, eggs and hash browns. Also cheese omelets, ham and cheese omelets, pancakes or French toast.

Burgers are big at Frenchy's with your choice of a 2/3 lb. or 1/3 lb. burger, bacon burgers and chili burgers. There's also tuna salads, ham, turkey, and roast beef sandwiches, club and grilled chicken sandwiches. Try the daily specials, and if you're just hanging out and enjoying the scenery, taste the chips and salsa or the nachos with chili.

While visiting the town of Tin Cup, take time to visit the old cemetery. It contains Protestant, Catholic and Jewish sections. The boot hill section was reserved for people who were shot with their boots on.

CONTACT US

Same owners as Frenchy's, own The Holts Guest Ranch in nearby Taylor Park
(979) 641-2733
(970) 642-0700
1711-13 CR 55, Almont, CO 81210

WHAT'S COOKING

American

HOW TO GET HERE

Tin Cup can be accessed from Cottonwood Pass west of Buena Vista, from Taylor Canyon east of Almont, and from the beautiful Cumberland Pass which exits from the north end of Pikin.

AREA ACTIVITIES

Fishing
Hunting
Snowmobiling
4 Wheeling
Mountain Biking
Kayaking
Cross Country Skiing
Climbing
Hiking

AREA INFORMATION

Tin Cup Colorado
www.pitkincolorado.com/tincup

Tin Cup Colorado Ghost Town
www.ghosttowns.com/tincup.html

Recipes

RED ROSE CAFÉ—PALISADE, COLORADO

CHICKEN ALMONDINE ALA PALISADE:

[Created in honor of the peach growing heritage of Palisade]

1] For each person: 1 4-6oz. boneless skinless chicken breast, lightly pounded to uniform thickness.
2] Coat with sliced almonds by dipping breast first in flour then egg wash then sliced almonds on both sides.
3] Sautee in oil until almonds are light brown then place in 400 degree oven to finish cooking.
4] For the sauce: For each serving. In a saucepan melt small pat of butter and a generous teaspoon of peach jam or preserves [in season add fresh sliced peaches]. When butter is melted finish with dash of peach schnapps. Pour sauce over chicken.

SALMON, TUNA OR SWORDFISH MEDITERRANEAN

[Great on the BBQ outdoors]
1] 8oz. steak either Salmon, Swordfish or Tuna.
Mediterranean Sauce:
2 Tbls. Extra virgin olive oil.
2 Roma Tomatoes diced.
1/2 Tbls. Capers.
1 Tbls. Fresh chopped herbs, basil, thyme, oregano and parsley.
1 Tbls. Fresh squeezed lemon juice and a splash of white wine.
2] Coat fish filets with olive oil and salt and pepper and grill to preferred temperature.
3] Place over chopped lettuce & top with sauce.

THE INN AT ARROWHEAD—CIMMARON, COLORADO

TRADITIONAL ENGLISH FISH & CHIPS:

[Their mum's recipe handed down to her from her mother and her mother before her]

Cod or Pollack Fillets.
Batter:
2 cups flour.
1 cup cornmeal.
1/2 cup honey corn bread mix [optional].
2 tsp. baking powder.
Method: Mix with a good hearty beer to make batter [Bass, Harp or Guinness are best]. Dip fish in seasoned flour, dip in batter. Deep fry till golden brown. Serve with chips [steak fries], green peas, and coleslaw.
Don't forget the malt vinegar.

OLD GERMANY RESTAURANT—DOLORES, COLORADO

GERMAN STYLE MEATLOAF:

5lbs. ground pork.
1 lb. ground beef.
1 onion, diced and sautéed.
1 cup of dried parsley.
Tbsp. white pepper.
1/2 Tbsp. black pepper.
1 Tbsp. salt.
1 pinch of nutmeg.
2 cups of breadcrumbs.
2 teasp. of garlic powder.
2 eggs.
2 packages of brown gravy mix.
2 1/2 cups of milk.

Method: Mix all together, form 3 loaves and bake in oven with 1/2 inch of water in bottom of pan for about 2 hrs. on 350 degrees or until the center of loaf reaches 160 degrees. Serve with brown gravy and mashed potatoes and purple cabbage.

SPRUCE LODGE RESORT—GRAND MESA , COLORADO

OVER THE TOP CHEESECAKE:

Preheat oven to 350
Crust: 2 cups graham cracker crumbs [finely crushed].
1 cube melted butter.
Combine and form into the bottom of a spring form pan sprayed with Pam Spray.

Filling: 2 pounds cream cheese [beat till creamy] and add.
1 cup sugar or honey.
2 eggs.
1/2 tsp. vanilla.
1/2 tsp. almond extract.
Beat till creamy and pour crust. Bake at 350 for 30 minutes.

Topping: 2 cups sour cream.
1/3 cup sugar.
1/2 tsp. almond extract.
Juice of 1/2 lemon.
Blend.

Method: Pour slowly over baked cheesecake and bake for 8 more minutes. Cool in refrigerator before serving. Drizzle with favorite topping, i.e., raspberry sauce, fresh fruit, or light caramel sauce with chopped pecans.

BUTCH'S LOBSTER BAR—SNOWMASS VILLAGE, COLORADO

SHANNON'S SHRIMP:

[serves 2]
Ingredients:
12 jumbo shrimp 15 ct. peeled and deveined, tails optional.
Flour seasoned with salt and pepper.
Egg Batter.
Clarified butter.
1 teaspoon whole butter.
1 teaspoon minced shallots.
1/2 teaspoon finely minced garlic.
1 ounce White Vermouth.
1 teaspoon Dijon mustard.
1/4 cup shrimp stock.*
1 teaspoon fresh parsley.
1 cup heavy whipping cream.
*Shrimp Stock:
Shrimp shells, 2 quarts cold water, 1/2 teaspoon Old Bay Seasoning, 1/4 cup white wine.

Method:
1] Shrimp Stock: Rinse shrimp shells in hot water. Place in a three-quart pot. Add cold water. Bring to a boil. Reduce heat and simmer. Season with Old Bay seasoning and white wine. Strain broth to produce shrimp stock. Boil to reduce by half. Should make about 1 pint.
2] Dredge shrimp in flour seasoned with salt and

pepper.
3] Dip shrimp in egg batter.
4] Saute in clarified butter in pre heated pan. Butter should sizzle when shrimp enters pan. Brown shrimp slightly, flip over and brown on other side.
5] Remove from pan and set aside.
6] Add 1 teaspoon of whole butter in pan. Saute shallots and garlic until translucent.
7] Deglaze with White Vermouth until reduced by half. Add Dijon, shrimp stock and cream.
8] Return shrimp to pan. Continue to reduce by half until bubbly. Add fresh parsley.
9] Serve on top or with rice and your favorite vegetable. May also be served with pasta or mashed potatoes.

THE GRILL BAR AND CAFÉ—LEADVILLE, COLORADO

CAPTAIN MARTINEZ RUM DRINK:

Regular: Use Captain Morgan Spiced Rum.
Dark: Use Captain Morgan Tattoo Rum.

Method: 10 oz. Rocks glass add ice, then pour a generous 2 oz. of rum. Generously squeeze fresh lemons, limes and finish with a quality Ginger Ale. Nice, Light and Refreshing.

WHITE BUFFALO WEST—BATTLEMENT MESA, COLORADO

GREEK SALAD:

[Yield: 20-25 Salads]

Marinate Ingredients:
4 - cups "Kraft Free" Italian dressing.
4 - cups olive oil.
2 - cups red wine vinegar.
1 - cup lemon juice.
6 - tbsp. oregano.
2 - tbsp. basil.
2 - tbsp. fresh garlic.
1 - tbsp. black pepper.
1 - tea. salt.
1 - bunch parsley, freshly minced.
2 - bunches green onions, diced thin.
1 - tea. cayenne.
Mix all ingredients and chill.

Salad:
10 - Cucumbers, quartered lengthwise and cubed.
10 - Tomatoes, diced large.
6 - Red onions, diced large.
Mix in bowl with dressing, then put the mix on top of salad lettuce, and top with Feta Cheese, Pepperoncinis and Greek Olives.

PINE CREEK COOKHOUSE—ASHCROFT, COLORADO

JACK DANIELS MARINATED CARIBOU, WITH SWEET POTATO:

Lasagna:

[Yields 4]
Caribou Marinade:
1/2- cup Jack Daniels.
1/4 - cup sweet soy sauce.
1/3 - cup red wine vinegar.
1/4 - cup mirin.
1 - tblsp. brown sugar.
1 - tblsp. green Tabasco.
1 - shallot chopped.
2 - pieces garlic sliced.
2 - tsp. pickled ginger chopped rough.
1/4 - cup honey.
4 - 6oz. pieces of Caribou.

Method: Combine all the ingredients except for the Caribou, mix well.
Add the Caribou to the marinade and let sit for at least 2 hours but no more than 24 hours.

PINE CREEK COOKHOUSE:

SWEET POTATO LASAGNA:

Method: Preheat oven to 400°.
With a mandoline slice the sweet potatoes into very thin rounds, dry the potatoes. Start in the center of the pan, overlapping slightly in a
spiral going clockwise. Sprinkle with salt , pepper, shallots, rosemary and thyme. Drizzle with clarified butter and repeat this until the potatoes are one.
Place in the oven for 45 minutes and check for doneness in the center of the lasagna with a fork.
Remove from pan and drain onto a paper towel.
Grill the caribou on medium high for 2 1/2 minutes on each side for rare, 4 minutes for medium rare.
Let stand for 2 minutes before you serve. Note wild game is best served rare, or medium rare, this is the most you should cook this cut because it loses it's flavor and texture because of the lack of marbling in this meat, it is very dense.
Sweet Potato Lasagna:

3 - lbs. sweet potatoes.
1/2 - lb. clarified butter.
1 - shallot diced.
1 - sprig thyme chopped.
1 - sprig rosemary chopped.
salt.
pepper.

RIVERS RESTAURANT—GLENWOOD SPRINGS, COLORADO

PISTACHIO CRÈME BRULEE WITH CARAMELIZED RASPBERRIES:

[Makes 4 3/4 Cup servings]

Preheat oven at 375 degrees.
2 Cups heavy cream.
1/4 Cup honey.
1/4 tsp. Vanilla extract.
Bring to a boil and simmer for 2 minutes.
4 Egg yolks.
1/4 Cup sugar.
Mix sugar and egg yolks together, temper cream mixture egg and cream mixture and mix thoroughly.
1 oz. Pistachio, chopped.
1 oz. Coarse grain sugar.
1 Cup Raspberries, fresh or frozen.

Method:
Divide chopped pistachio into 4 oven proof cups [soufflé cups], pour Crème Brulee mixture over chopped pistachios and place soufflé cups into a pan with a water bath. Bake at 375° for approximately 45 minutes, or until the custard is set. Remove from water pan and let cool. Top each Crème Brulee evenly with 1/4 cup raspberries and sugar, flame with a torch or place under broiler to caramelize sugar. Let cool prior to serving.

BRANDING IRON STEAKHOUSE—CRAWFORD, COLORADO

EASY CHEESE CAKE:

Graham Cracker Crust:
1 1/2 cups of crushed Graham Crackers.
1/4 cup of sugar.
1/2 cup melted butter.
Method:
Preheat oven to 350 degrees. Put butter into 13x9x2 in. pan and melt in oven. Mix well the Graham Cracker crumbs and sugar in a bowl with a spoon. Empty the Graham Cracker mixture into the melted butter pan and spread to the edges of the pan with a fork. Put the crust into the oven for 8 to 10 min. or until light golden brown. Let cool.

Cheese Cake:
8 oz. of Cream Cheese.
1/2 cup of sugar.
2 tsp. of vanilla.
8 oz. of sour cream.
8 oz. of whipped topping [already mixed]
Method:
Mix all ingredients together until well blended, pour on top of the Graham Cracker crust. Top with your favorite fruit topping. Chill for 1 hour.

DUNTON HOT SPRINGS—DUNTON, COLORADO

DOUG'S SMOTHERED LAMB:

1 lb. Boned shoulder lamb, cut in inch dices.
1 small onion, chopped.
1 piece of ginger.
1 medium tomato.
1/2 cup chopped cilantro.
1 or 2 chilies cut into rings.
1/4 tsp. ground tumeric.
2 tsp. garam masala.
1 tsp. ground cumin.
1/4 cup plain yogurt.
1 tbl. tomato paste.
Salt.
3 tbl. vegetable oil.
4 cloves chopped garlic.

Method:
Put oil, garlic and pepper in big pot, cook until light brown. Now put remaining ingredients in seasoned meat and stir once, cover and cook until meat falls apart and juices are reduced.

DOUBLE CHOCOLATE COOKIES:

2 cups flour.
1/2 cup Dutch-pressed cocoa.
2 tsp. baking powder.
1 tsp. salt.
1 6oz. semi sweet chocolate, chopped.
4 large eggs.
2 tsp. vanilla extract.
10 tbl. butter softened but firm.
1 1/2 cups brown sugar.
1/2 cup granulated sugar.

Method:
Sift together flour, cocoa, baking powder, and salt in medium bowl and set aside. Melt chocolate in top double stirring until smooth. Beat eggs and vanilla and set aside. Beat butter until creamy, beat in sugars until combined and gradually beat in eggs. Add chocolate in steady stream and mix scrapings sides of bowl. Add flour mixture, stir until combined. DO NOT over blend. Cover and let stand for 30 minutes. Pre heat oven to 350·, bake cookies until edges just begin to set. You can also add 12oz. of white chocolate chips with the flour mixture if you want

ROASTED VEGETABLE AND TOMATO SOUP:

5-10 lbs. tomatoes and or roasted vegetables.
Garlic to taste.
2 onions peeled and cut into large pieces.
2-3 bunches fresh thyme.
1 or 2 jalapeno peppers.
Olive oil.
Chicken stock.
Cream.

Method:
Cut out stems of tomatoes and place in roasting pan, put garlic into each cut on tomato, add onions, pepper and thyme to pan. Drizzle with olive oil, add salt and pepper and roast 2-5 hours. Remove skin from tomatoes, add all remaining ingredients to blender and blend until smooth, doing batches until veggie are all blended. Heat through and add cream and season.

THE REDSTONE INN—REDSTONE, COLORADO

REDSTONE INN'S CREAM OF ARTICHOKE WITH CHICKEN:

1 1/2 cups yellow onions, diced 1/4 inch.
1 1/2 cups celery, diced 1/4 inch.
1/2 cup olive oil.
1 cup all purpose flour.
2 lbs. [cooked weight] chicken meat, cooked and diced.
1 Quarts canned artichoke hearts, quartered.
1/2 cup roasted garlic cloves, minced.
2 Quarts heavy whipping cream.
2 Quarts chicken stock.
2 tsp. white pepper.
2 tb. dried basil.
salt to taste.

Method:
In a heavy bottom soup or stock pot over medium heat sauté onions and celery in olive oil until translucent. Add flour and continue cooking. Stir constantly until flour changes to a blond color. You now have a roux which will be what thickens the soup. Add remaining ingredients and bring to a simmer. Cook only until soup thickens, stirring often as cream soups scorch easily. Adjust salt and seasonings. You can serve this soup with a little grated cheddar or Parmesan on top, or a dash of olive oil or pesto.

REDSTONE INN'S SCALLION MASHED POTATOES:

5 lbs. Yukon Gold potatoes, peeled and diced to 1 inch.
1 cup scallions [greentops only] coarsely chopped.
1 cup milk.
1 cup heavy cream.
1/2 lb. butter
1 tsp. white pepper.
1 tbl. salt.

Method:
Place potatoes in four to five quarts of lightly salted water and bring to a low boil until potatoes are tender. Place scallions and milk in a bar blender and blend until a uniform green color. Combine cream, milk/scallion mixture, butter, white pepper and salt in a sauce pan and bring to a simmer. Drain potatoes and run through a food mill or use a potato masher. Place mashed potatoes and hot cream into a mixing bowl, use a counter top or hand held mixer. Mix on medium high for about 30 seconds, then scrape the bowl and mix for another 30 seconds. If you have a few scallions left sprinkle them on top at service.

THE REDSTONE INN'S SUNDRIED CHERRY VINAIGRETTE:

This is a mildly sweet dressing that can be served at room temperature, tossed with fresh spinach, diced granny smith apples, toasted pine nuts and warm goat cheese. The dressing can be heated if you prefer a more wilted salad. Grilled duck or chicken would also work well as additions to the salad. Pecans or walnuts may be used in lieu of pine nuts.

2 cups dried tart cherries.
1 cup red wine vinegar.
2 cups salad or olive oil.
1/2 cups honey.
1/2 cup plum sauce.
1/2 cup Dijon.
1 1/2 tsp. salt.
1 tsp. salt.
1 tsp. black pepper.

Method:
Combine all ingredients and allow to sit for approximately 30 minutes. Remove half of dressing to a blender and puree. Re-combine ingredients and mix well. Add salt to taste.

LA CHAUMIERE LYONS, COLORADO

SAUTEED ROCKY MOUNTAIN TROUT LA CHAUMIERE:

[4 servings]

4 fresh trout, 10 oz. boneless.
1 tablespoon fresh parsley.
juice of 2 lemons.
1/2 cup of peeled canned green grapes.
1/2 cup blanced sliced almonds.
salt and pepper to taste.
1/2 cup olive oil.
1 cup heavy cream.
1 cup flour.

Method:
Place the cream in a large platter or cookie sheet. Lay the trout meat side down into the cream. Let rest in the cream for 15 minutes. Heat large skillet and add olive oil. Dredge the trout in the flour and place in the hot skillet, meat side down. Add grapes. Brown on both sides, season with salt and ground black pepper the add lemon juice, place almonds on top. Place in a 400-degree oven for 2 to 3 minutes. Remove from the oven, place on a platter and garnish with parsley.

DANDELION SOUP:

1 head iceberg lettuce.
1 1/2 cup dandelion greens [use only the young tender greens
washed and cleaned].
1/4 cup onions, chopped.
1/2 cup chopped parsley.
1 gallon chicken stock.

Method:
Place chicken stock, parsley, onion, dandelion greens and lettuce into a large stockpot. Bring to a boil and simmer for 15 minutes. Add 1 cup of roux [roux consist of equal parts flour and butter. Melt the butter and add flour]. After adding the roux let it cook for about 5 minutes and it will thicken slightly. Remove from heat and puree in blender or food processor. Upon reheating add half and half to taste for added richness. Adjust seasoning with salt and ground white pepper to taste.

LAVENDER CRUSTED POUSSIN:

1 young roasting chicken [2 to 2 1/2 pounds].
Salt and Pepper to taste.
1/4 cup herbs de provence.
1/4 olive oil.
1/2 cup dried lavender.
1 roll of butcher string.

Method:
Start by boning the chicken starting at the back bone. Start by placing the chicken breast side down. Start by cutting on each side of the backbone or request the butcher prepare the chicken. Placing skin side down rubbing the meat side with olive oil and sprikle with salt and pepper and herbs de provence. Roll into cylinder shape and tie with the butcher string, rub the skin with olive oil and season with salt and pepper and dust with lavender. Place in a preheated oven at 375-degrees and cook until the internal temperature is 160-degrees. Remove from the oven and let stand for 10 minutes. Cut the strings and slice and place on a platter. Here at La Chaumiere we prepare a light glaze to serve with our Lavender Crusted Chicken. It is prepared by using 3/4 cup apricot juice and 1/4 cup srong chicken stock, heat the ingrediants and place over the chicken. just before serving.

THE ANTLERS RIO GRANDE LODGE & RIVERSIDE RESTAURANT
CREEDE, COLORADO

HERB MARINATED ELK LOIN WITH MOREL SAUCE:

[serves 4]

4 6-80z. trimmed elk strip loins.
1 teaspoons chopped rosemary.
2 teaspoons chopped garlic.
1 tablespoon Dijon mustard.

1 dash Worcestershire sauce.
1/4 cup olive oil.
Salt & Pepper to taste.

Mix above ingredients and rub on elk. Let sit for 24 hours in refrigerator.Sear in hot skillet and finish in the oven to desired temperature.

For Morel Sauce:
4 oz. dried Morels.
2 cups of Veal Demi Glaze.
2-3 oz. of Brandy.
1 cup heavy cream.
2 tablespoons chopped shallots.
1 tablespoon garlic.

Method:
Soak Morels in water until rehydrated and chop. Sautee shallots, garlic and chopped morels. Deglaze with brandy and add demi-glaze & cream. Simmer for 5 minutes, add salt & pepper to taste.

CHALET SWISS, SOUTH FORK, COLORADO

PORK LOIN IN BEER SAUCE:

16 oz. pork loin, trimmed, cut into 1" slices.
1 tablespoon cooking oil.
1/2 teaspoon salt.
1 teaspoon paprika [preferably Hungarian].
1 teaspoon all purpose flour'
1 garlic clove, finely minced.
1/2 onion, finely chopped.
zest of 1/2 lemon.
chopped fresh parsley to garnish.
1/2 teaspoon cumin seeds.
Sauce:
8 oz. of beer [any blonde beer].
1 teaspoon of chicken broth.
4 oz. water.
4 oz. of heavy cream or half and half.

Method:
Heat cooking oil on medium heat, add pork loin and thoroughly sear, about 6 minutes. Add salt, paprika, garlic, onion, lemon zest, cumin seeds, and flour stirring well to avoid lumps. Allow to simmer for another 6 minutes, till meat is fully cooked and tender. Remove from heat and transfer to another container, cover dish to keep warm.
Using the same pan, add beer and de-glaze pan at high heat, let beer reduce to half. Mix chicken broth with water and ad to beer. Let simmer until sauce is well incorporated. Add cream or half and half, bring to a light boil. Add pork loin mixture and let simmer. Add salt and pepper to taste. Serve over pasta, rice or mashed potatoes [spaetzle would be best!]; Garnish with parsley and cumin seeds. Bon Appetit!

POPPIES BISTRO CAFÉ– ASPEN, COLORADO

SAUTED PHEASANT BREAST WITH BALSAMIC CREAM SAUCE:

2-6 oz. Pheasant Breast.
1/4 - Cup White Wine.
1/4-Cup Balsamic Vinegar.
1/8-Raspbery Vinegar.
1/8-Cup Cassis.
Pinch of Shallots.
Pinch of Garlic.
1/2-Cup Chicken Stock.
1/2-Cup Heavy Cream.
Salt and Pepper, to Taste.
1/4-Cup Chicken Stock.

Method:
Preheat oven to 375 degrees. In a hot sautė pan, put in enough clariefied butter to coat the pan. Cook the pheasant skin side down. When browned, turn over and brown the other side. Put in 1/2 cup chicken broth. When it comes to a boil, put the pan and all of its contents into the 375 degree oven for approximatly 10 minutes. While the pheasant is cooking, make the sauce.

Method for Sauce:
In a sauce pot, combine wine, both vinegars, cassis, shallot and garlic. Bring to a boil over high heat until reduced to a glaze. Add the 1/4 cup chicken stock and bring to a boil and cook for 3 minutes. Add the heavy cream and return to a boil. Cook over medium heat until the desired sauce consistency, approximately 4 to 5 minutes.

To Serve:
When the pheasant is done, remove from the pan, reserve the pan and its drippings. Slice the pheasant thin. Fan nicely on the serving plates.
Add the sauce to the drippings in the sautė pan and bring to a boil. Pour over the sliced pheasant.

SWEETWATER MYSTERY COOKIES:

1 lb. Butter
1 Cup Sugar
1 Teaspoon Vanilla Extract
3 1/2 Cups Flour
2 Cups Potato Chips, crushed
1/2 Cups Pecan
1 Cup Coconut

Method:
Cream together butter and sugar, add vanilla and stir in flour. Add potato chips, nuts and coconut. Scoop by teaspoon onto a greased cookie sheet. Bake at 350 degrees for 15 minutes.
Delicious with fresh peaches over the top.

CRYSTAL LODGE AND RESTAURANT:

CRAB AND BOURSIN STUFFED RUBY RED TROUT:

4 7oz. Ruby red trout filets
10 oz. Lump crab meat
4 oz. Boursin wheel
2 Cups heavy cream
Salt and pepper to taste
Fresh herbs and finely diced red bell pepper [garnish]

Method:
Reduce heavy cream by half and the add 1/4 of the Boursin wheel over low to medium heat for 4 minutes. Salt and pepper to taste. Lightly grill trout on flesh side for 2 to 4 minutes. Place in oven safe dish and top

THE REDSTONE INN'S AHI NACHOS:

1 Lbs. Ahi Tuna.
1 cup Light Soy Sauce.
1/2 cup Sesame Oil [pure]
1/2 cup Rice wine vinagar.
1/ tsp. Cayenne.
2 Tbl. Sesame seeds.
2 Tbl. Picked Ginger, juliienne.
Sushi grade Ahi tuna is not necessary for this recipe, #2 grade as long as it is fresh, works fine and tends to be much less expensive. The recipe can be easily cut in half or expanded. As a gauge 1 lb. of tuna is probably enough for ten people. The marinade can be stored refrigerated for several days but don't marinade the fish more than four or five hours before you intend to serve it. Yes the fish is served raw but the marinade "cooks" it much like seviche.

Method:
Remove skin if present and dice Ahi to 3/8 to 1/2 inch cubes.
In a 2 qt. bowl, combine soy, sesame oil, vinegar, cayenne, sesame seeds, and ginger. Mix well with a whisk.
Add Ahi to bowl, mix well, cover with plastic wrap or lid. Allow fish to marinate for 2 to 4 hours, a hard and fast rule for how long to marinate it is impossible but three hours is generally sufficient.

Wasabi: 1/2 cup.
Water: approximately 1/2 cup water.
Combine water and wasabi mix well, add water to desired consistency.

Chips:
Egg roll, or spring roll wrappers: 1 lb. pkg.
Cut wrappers in stacks of five or six sheets to desired size [we cut ours in about 1/2 in. squares but other shapes will work as well.
Separate the cut stacks into individual pieces.
Deep fry in vegetable oil or shortening, in a Fry Daddy or shallow sauce pan. [follow the same precautions used when frying any food, oil is hot!].
Remove from oil and drain on paper towels.

At service time: [Which should be no more than ten or fifteen minutes before they are intended to be eaten]. Place chips on cookie sheet. Drain Ahi in a colander, and place a serving [a little more than a teaspoon but a little less than a tablespoon is about the best description] on each chip. Using a spoon or squeeze bottle, drizzle Wasabi over 'Nachos". [The wasabi recipe given above makes for a consistency that should resemble mustard, adjust water or wasabi as needed]. Go easy on the drizzle but have some wasabi available for your friends that want more "kick". Place on a serving tray or plate, serve at room temperature. The "nachos" my be garnished with finely diced red bell peppers and/or green onion julienne, radish sprouts.

THE REDSTONE INN'S ELK IN PHYLLO:

1 lb. Elk*
1/3 cup olive oil.
2 tbls. shallots minced.
2 tbls. roasted and minced garlic cloves.
1 cup sliced mushrooms.
1/2 tsp. black pepper.
1/2 tsp. salt
1 1/2 cups fresh spinach, cleaned and chopped 1/2 inch.
3/4 cup goat cheese, crumbled.
3/4 cup pine nuts [roasted].
* Elk venison or even lamb will interchange in this recipe.

Method:
Clean meat of fat and silver, dice into 1/2 inch cubes.
In a very hot pan place enough oil to cover bottom.
Then immedietly add shallots and garlic. Reduce heat to medium.
Stir until shallots turn translucent and are starting to brown.
Add meat and sauté to browned, stir often.
Add mushrooms and continue to stir till mushrooms are cooked.
Add remaining ingredients except goat cheese, and continue to cook until spinach is cooked, add goat cheese and fold in.
Remove from heat and allow to cool.
Pour off any excess liquid.

To make purses, portion filling into 3 1/2 ounce portions, wrap in plastic wrap and freeze. If just filling cups, you may serve directly.

For The Purses:

1 1lb. Pkg. Frozen Phyllo Dough.
1/4 Lb. Butter.
1 ea. Egg.

Method:
Follow directions on the phyllo package for working with phyllo. Layer five sheets brushed with melted butter between the sheets. Cut sheets into six portions, place a frozen portion of filling into center of each phyllo square. Pull corners of phyllo up and form into a purse. Pinch the purse closed tighly against the top of the filling leaving top edges of the phyllo to splay out a little bit. Prepare an egg wash by mixing egg with 1/4 cup of water. Brush finished purses with egg wash.
Purses may be prepared a day in advance and refrigerated. Do not cover during refrigeration, a little corn meal sprinkled on the bottom of the storage container keeps the purses from sticking during storage.
To serve, pre-heat oven to 425 degrees, bake purses on lightly buttered or sprayed sheet pan and bake phyllo 10-12 minutes. Or until golden brown.
We serve ours on a demi glace based, roasted shallot sauce and garnish with goat cheese and fried sage.
Prepared or reconstituted demi glaze is available in

most grocery stores. To make the sauce roast or sauté diced shallots until they are a dark brown, use about 1 tablespoon per cup of demi glaze the shallots may be deglazed with red wine, sherry or port for a little more zip. Blend warm demi glaze and shallots in a counter top blender till the sauce has a smooth texture, and salt and pepper to taste. One cup of sauce should be enough for this recipe as only about a tablespoon is placed under the finished "purse". The sauce should be served warm.
If available fresh chives can be tied around the neck where the purse is pinched together. Fried sage is made by picking fresh sage from the stems and frying in olive oil or peanut oil until crispy.

THE WIT'S END GUEST RANCH-LAKE VALLECITO, COLORADO

COLORADO LAMB RACK WITH CHERRY CHUTNEY:

1 Each Colorado lamb rack.
1 Tsp. Honey.
1 Tsp. Dijon mustard.
1 Tsp. Rosemary, finely chopped.
1 Tsp. Basil, finely chopped.
1 Tsp. Parsley, finely chopped.
Salt and Pepper to taste.

Method:
Sear off the lamb until deep golden brown and let cool for 10 min. Mix the honey and Dijon together and coat the loin front and back.Chop herbs separately then combine them after finely chopped. Coat the loin with the herbs.
Pre heat oven to 350, bake on a sheet pan for 25 to 30 min. or until desired temperature is met. Chefs choice is medium rare, 130 degrees internal temperature.

Red Chili Cherry Chutney:

4 cloves garlic finely chopped.
2 Tsp. Olive oil.
1 1/2 cups onions finely chopped.
1 cup orange juice.
1 cup aged sherry vinegar.
1/4 cup balsamic vinegar.
1 1/4 cup lite brown sugar.
1 Tbs. Chipolte in adobo finely chopped.
1/8 Tsp. ground cumin.
1/2 Tsp. ground cinnamon.

Method:
Heat olive oil, sauté onions on medium heat for about 5 mins.Add orange juice, vinegars and sugar, bring to a boil, stir until sugar dissolves. Reduce to about 2 cups. Add cinnamon, Chipotle, cumin, cherries and garlic and reduce it until it resembles a thin syrup. Let it cool at room temperature.

GRILLED SEA BASS WITH ORANGE COCONUT CURRY SAUCE:

[Yields 4 servings]

2 Whole Sea Bass.
2 Tbls. Chopped basil.
1 oz. Olive oil.
Salt and Pepper.

Orange Coconut Curry Sauce:
3 Large basil leaves.
2 Cans of coconut milk.
1 Orange, pealed and chopped.
3 Garlic cloves, chopped.
1.5 Tea. green curry paste. 1/2 Cup orange juice,
1 Tea. Canola oil.

Method:
Marinate fish in 2 Tbls. of chopped basil and 1 oz. olive oil.
Sweat shallots in oil for 30 seconds, add curry paste, orange and basil leaves, and simmer for 3 mins.
Add lemon grass, ginger, garlic and coconut milk, simmer for 20 mins.
Strain and season with salt and pepper.